MACMILLAN **ACADEMIC SKILLS**

Skillful
Listening&Speaking

Teacher's Book

4

Author: Louis Rogers
Series Consultant: Dorothy E. Zemach

Macmillan Education
4 Crinan Street
London N1 9XW
A division of Macmillan Publishers Limited
Companies and representatives throughout the world

ISBN 978-0-230-43011-2

Written by Louis Rogers

First published 2014

Note to Teachers

Designed by emc design limited

Cover design by emc design limited

Page make-up by MPS Limited

The Academic Keyword List (AKL) was designed by Magali Paquot at the Centre for English Corpus Linguistics, Université catholique de Louvain (Belgium) within the framework of a research project led by Professor Sylviane Granger.

http://www.uclouvain.be/en-372126.html

Author's acknowledgements
I'd like to thank everyone involved in the project for making *Skillful* such a great series.

Please see Student's Book imprint page for visual walkthrough photo credits.

Printed and bound in Thailand

2018 2017 2016 2015 2014
10 9 8 7 6 5 4 3 2 1

Contents

Map of Student's Book

		Listening texts	Critical thinking skills	Language development
UNIT 1	**Gathering** Page 7	1 Three meetings 🇺🇸🇬🇧 2 Getting from *you and me*, to *we* 🇬🇧	Inferring a speaker's attitude Applying a theory to other situations	Binomials Modal verbs and levels of directness
UNIT 2	**Games** Page 17	1 Video games: Lessons for life 🇬🇧 2 Game theory 🇺🇸	Identifying key information in an argument Selecting information for notes and summaries	Prepositional verbs Phrasal verbs
UNIT 3	**Nostalgia** Page 27	1 How to deal with homesickness 🇺🇸🇬🇧 2 Memory and smell 🇬🇧	Organizing qualitative data Representative samples	Approximation Particulizer and exclusive adverbs
UNIT 4	**Risk** Page 37	1 The world's most dangerous jobs 🇺🇸 2 What is acceptable risk? 🇺🇸	Using illustrative examples to support an argument Anticipating a conclusion based on reasons and evidence	Nominalization Possible, probable, and hypothetical future predictions
UNIT 5	**Sprawl** Page 47	1 Cars and cities 🇺🇸 2 Making cities more liveable 🇬🇧	Recognizing logical order Evaluating against criteria	Connotation Academic verbs
UNIT 6	**Legacy** Page 57	1 Family food legacies 🇺🇸 2 Technology legacies 🇺🇸🇬🇧	Source validity Use of the passive in source citations	Inversion Collocations: *way*
UNIT 7	**Expanse** Page 67	1 The Trans-Siberian Railway 🇺🇸🇬🇧 2 Why do people climb mountains? 🇺🇸	Differentiating between fact and opinion Identifying statements that need justification	Attitude adverbials Abstract nouns
UNIT 8	**Change** Page 77	1 Metamorphosis—the secrets behind nature's amazing change 🇺🇸 2 A global tax on changing money? 🇬🇧	Maximizing language Recognizing implicit assumptions	Expressing change Gradable adjectives
UNIT 9	**Flow** Page 87	1 Not worth a dam 🇬🇧 2 The concept of flow 🇺🇸	Identifying counter-arguments Visual aids and diagrams	Irregular plurals Words in context— working with concordance data
UNIT 10	**Conflict** Page 97	1 Conflict of interest 🇬🇧 2 "The Sporting Spirit" 🇺🇸	Identifying strengths in theories and arguments Consistency	Hedging and boosting Using the correct linker

🇬🇧 = features British English;   🇺🇸 = features American English

Pronunciation skill	Speaking skill	Speaking task	Digibook video activity	Study skills & Critical thinking skills
Intonation and attitude	Interrupting	Planning a study group	No man is an island	Study skills: Speaking in groups
Identifying the linking /r/	Agreeing and disagreeing—degrees of formality	Formulating a debate on banning violent electronic games	Reality TV: The harsh reality	Critical thinking skills: Why develop critical thinking skills? *Stella Cottrell*
Juncture	Identifying sources of information	Conducting a survey on memory	Retro-volution	Study skills: Listening to extended lectures
Word stress in word families	Managing conversation	Undertaking an informal risk assessment	Risky business	Critical thinking skills: Critical thinking: Knowledge, skills, and attitudes *Stella Cottrell*
Contrastive stress	Supporting proposals	Presenting a proposal of an action plan for an urban issue	The urban footprint	Study skills: Recording achievement
Pausing for dramatic emphasis	Emphasizing important information—repetition and contrastive pairs	Making a speech about a person who has left a legacy	Tracing the family line	Critical thinking skills: The author's position *Stella Cottrell*
Word stress: abstract nouns formed from adjectives	Negotiating	Organizing a cultural program	Infinite boundaries	Study skills: Organizing your personal study online
Intonation and tonic prominence	Adding points to an argument	Holding a debate about educational changes	Shock to the system	Critical thinking skills: Argument and disagreement *Stella Cottrell*
Intonation to express hesitation and doubt	Softening criticism	Making an advertisement supported by visuals	Volcanic flow	Study skills: Exam techniques
Linking and catenation	Managing conflict—reformulating and monitoring	Role-playing mini-conflict situations	The warrior gene	Critical thinking skills: Categorising *Stella Cottrell*

VOCABULARY PREVIEW Pre-teaching essential vocabulary which appears in both texts within the unit.

BEFORE YOU LISTEN These introductions to the listening topics prepare students for the upcoming subject matter.

LISTENING
When students first hear the text, they are encouraged to engage with the big issues and the overall picture before moving on to a more detailed analysis.

Vocabulary preview

1 Circle the two synonyms in each group of words.

1	launch	withdrawal	unveil
2	to maintain	to revolutionize	to change the face of
3	to overlook	to address	to deal with
4	to hand down	to pass on	to withhold
5	achievement	flop	success
6	to convey	to conceal	to express
7	to stand to	to be likely to	to be unlikely to
8	routine	ritual	custom

2 Work with a partner. Discuss any difference in connotation between the synonyms. More than one answer might be possible.

3 Use the correct form of one of the synonyms in each row from exercise 1 to complete the sentences below.

1 The _____ of the iPhone changed the way people interact.
2 The Internet has _____ international communication.
3 The best way to _____ urban pollution is to ban private cars.
4 The best ideas are _____ from generation to generation.
5 The true measure of _____ is not money-related.
6 It is always best to _____ your ideas as simply as possible.
7 Banks that _____ make huge profits this year should donate some of the profits to charity.
8 Traditional _____ are dying out in most countries.

4 Do you agree or disagree with the above statements?

LISTENING 1 Family food legacies 🇺🇸

Before you listen

Discuss the following questions with a partner.

1 How often do you eat with your family?
   a 7 days a week   b 4–6 days a week   c 0–3 days a week
2 What advantages are there in eating together as a family? Is this common in your culture? Why or why not?
3 Who tends to prepare the meals in your family? Why is this?

Listening

1 🔊 2.04 Listen to a lecture on family food legacies. Take notes on the topic using these mind map headings.

Reasons for the decline in sharing meals — **Family food legacies** — *The positive effects of family meal times*

What can happen when people share a meal? *Examples of family food legacies*

CRITICAL THINKING SKILLS BOXES
These focus on new skills, giving information on why they are important and how to do them. They also highlight the linguistic features to look out for.

DEVELOPING CRITICAL THINKING
Developing critical thinking is a chance to reflect on issues presented in the text.

LISTENING TASKS
Providing the opportunity to put a new skill into practice.

---

2 Work with a partner and compare your mind maps. Do you agree with the information the speaker presented in the lecture?

Critical thinking skill

SOURCE VALIDITY

Remember that it is important to note sources of information (cf. p. 61). Citing sources in your presentation can give you more credibility. Likewise, you may need to critically assess other speakers' sources by asking yourself these questions:

- Does the source material actually exist?
- Does the speaker present the source material accurately?
- Is the citation from an authoritative source or from, e.g., an amateur blogger?
- Is the source material useful for my own research needs?
- Does/Did the source material make a recognized contribution to the area of study?
- Even if a primary source is cited, was the research valid? For example, if the research only used two participants, but makes sweeping statements about its findings, then it might not be valid.

ACADEMIC KEYWORDS

analysis   (n) /əˈnæləsɪs/
examine   (v) /ɪgˈzæmɪn/
strengthen   (v) /ˈstreŋθən/

1 🔊 2.04 Listen to the lecture again and complete the table below.

Information	Source name	Publication name	Primary (P)/ Secondary (S) source?	Authoritative source?	Valid research participant base?
		n/a		✓ *Anthropologist at Rutgers University, U.S.*	
			S		✓ *182,000 youngsters*
	Russell Belk	*"Sharing," Journal of Consumer Research, VoC*			
Rich and delicious memories connected to eating at home.		*Online forum*			
A ritual makes a family feel united.			S		

2 Which information from the chart above lacks validity? Which has stronger validity? What is missing from information that you would need to follow up? How would you set about following it up?

Developing critical thinking

Discuss these questions in a group.

1 Is sharing a meal a valuable way of teaching a person to be a member of a culture or society? Why or why not?
2 Why do you think so many of our traditions are centered around meals?
3 Go back to *Speaking skill* exercise 1 on page 54. Rank the extracts from most reliable (*1*) to least reliable (*4*). Give reasons for your choices.

Language development

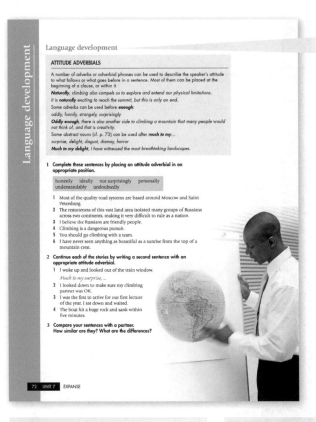

Language development

ATTITUDE ADVERBIALS

A number of adverbs or adverbial phrases can be used to describe the speaker's attitude to what follows or what goes before in a sentence. Most of them can be placed at the beginning of a clause, or within it.

Naturally, climbing also compels us to explore and extend our physical limitations.

It is *naturally* exciting to reach the summit, but this is only an end.

Some adverbs can be used before *enough*:

oddly, funnily, strangely, surprisingly

Oddly enough, there is also another side to climbing a mountain that many people would not think of, and that is creativity.

Some abstract nouns (cf. p. 73) can be used after **much to my**...

surprise, delight, disgust, dismay, horror

***Much to my delight**, I have witnessed the most breathtaking landscapes.*

1 Complete these sentences by placing an attitude adverbial in an appropriate position.

> honestly   ideally   not surprisingly   personally
> understandably   undoubtedly

1 Most of the quality road systems are based around Moscow and Saint Petersburg.
2 The remoteness of this vast land area isolated many groups of Russians across two continents, making it very difficult to rule as a nation.
3 I believe the Russians are friendly people.
4 Climbing is a dangerous pursuit.
5 You should go climbing with a team.
6 I have never seen anything as beautiful as a sunrise from the top of a mountain crest.

2 Continue each of the stories by writing a second sentence with an appropriate attitude adverbial.

1 I woke up and looked out of the train window.
   Much to my surprise, ...
2 I looked down to make sure my climbing partner was OK.
3 I was the first to arrive for our first lecture of the year. I sat down and waited.
4 The boat hit a huge rock and sank within five minutes.

3 Compare your sentences with a partner. How similar are they? What are the differences?

72   UNIT 7   EXPANSE

LANGUAGE DEVELOPMENT Notes on form and function appear in both Student's Books, and provide practice of key points.

SECTION OVERVIEW Giving students the context within which they are going to study the productive skills.

REAL-WORLD FOCUS The focus on real-world situations allows students to use these skills in discussion groups and seminars.

SKILLS BOXES Highlighting pronunciation advice.

Speaking skills

SPEAKING Presenting a proposal of an action plan for an urban issue

You are going to practice expressing opinions in order to put your ideas across with sufficient support and examples. You will also learn how to identify and use contrastive stress. Then you are going to use these skills to present a proposal for an action plan for an urban issue.

Pronunciation skill

CONTRASTIVE STRESS

Stress on certain words in a sentence can be used to indicate contrast between two things or to correct previous information. When you are contrasting two ideas or concepts, the stress should fall on both noun or gerund phrases, to highlight the differences through intonation as well as meaning.

Unlike some livability ranking data this award doesn't focus on salaries, it focuses on well-being.

While banning cars from our city centers would be one solution, improving cycling facilities would be a more positive step.

1 Predict where the contrastive stress will fall in these sentences.

1 Our current city planning isn't only about architecture; it also includes green spaces.
2 New Delhi isn't India's largest city; it's the largest metropolitan area.
3 If parks are the lungs, then water is the blood of a city!

2 2.01 Listen and check.

3 Write three untrue sentences about your partner. Your partner will correct the information using contrastive stress.

Speaking skill

SUPPORTING PROPOSALS

When making proposals or explaining a plan of action, it is important to put your ideas across with sufficient support and examples. Here are some ways to do this effectively.

Supporting your proposal with a reason
I say this because ...   Let me explain why / the reasons for ...   The reason is ...   One reason for ...

Giving examples
For instance ...   For example ...   Let me give you a clear example ...   As an example ...

Referring to generally held beliefs / common sense
These expressions can also be used to restate/reformulate ideas (cf. p. 104).
It's obvious that ...   It makes sense to ...   As we all know ...   Common sense tells us ...

1 2.02 Listen to four extracts. What problems are being discussed? What solution is proposed?

2 Propose solutions to these problems with a partner.
• There are too many delegates on the initial conference invitation list.
• You will not be able to finish a report before the deadline.

54   UNIT 5   SPRAWL

SPEAKING TASK

BRAINSTORM
You are going to plan and present a proposal for an action plan for an urban-related issue. In a proposal, you identify a problem and state how you will solve that problem.
With a partner, make a list of common urban problems connected to the categories below. Think of reasons for these problems, and provide evidence or examples of how these problems effect city dwellers.

green areas   housing   pollution   population   retail areas   traffic

PLAN
Choose one of the problems from the brainstorm stage. Plan a proposal to deal with the problem. A proposal format identifies a problem, states the effect of the problem, and then proposes a solution to the problem, with reasons and evidence. A strong proposal is based on factual information rather than opinion.

SPEAK
Find other pairs who chose the same problem as you. Present your proposal to those pairs. Remember to give reasons and evidence. Also remember to support your arguments, using appropriate language. (Don't forget to also try and practice some of the previously-learned skills: stress, intonation, using academic verbs, nominalization, and particulizer and exclusive adverbs.) Listen to the other speakers' proposals, ask questions, and make comments.

SHARE
As a whole class, discuss the various proposed solutions you have heard. Which proposals were presented well and could be made into a campaign video to be forwarded to a relevant group?

SPRAWL   UNIT 5   55

AUDIO MATERIALS Providing guided practice.

GUIDED PRACTICE Guides students through the stages of a speaking task.

CRITICAL THINKING SKILLS WITH STELLA COTTRELL

At the end of each unit, there is either a study skills focus, or a focus on an aspect of critical thinking. The critical thinking pages showcase a theme from Stella Cottrell's bestselling book *Critical Thinking Skills*.

EXPLANATION BOXES

These provide a clear explanation of what the focus is.

Critical thinking skills

Why develop critical thinking skills?

by Stella Cottrell

Benefits of critical thinking skills

Good critical thinking skills bring numerous benefits such as:

- improved attention and observation;
- more focused reading;
- improved ability to identify the key points in a text or other message rather than becoming distracted by less important material;
- improved ability to respond to the appropriate points in a message;
- knowledge of how to get your own point across more easily;
- skills of analysis that you can choose to apply in a variety of situations.

Benefits in professional and everyday life

Skills in critical thinking bring precision to the way you think and work. You will find that practice in critical thinking helps you to be more accurate and specific in noting what is relevant and what is not. The skills listed above are useful to problem-solving and to project management, bringing greater precision and accuracy to different parts of a task.

Although critical thinking can seem like a slow process because it is precise, once you have acquired good skills, they save you time because you learn to identify the most relevant information more quickly and accurately.

Ancillary skills

Critical thinking involves the development of a range of ancillary skills such as:

- observation
- reasoning
- decision-making
- analysis
- judgement
- persuasion

Realistic self-appraisal

It is likely that you already possess some or all of these skills in order to cope with everyday life, work or previous study. However, the more advanced the level of study or the professional area, the more refined these skills need to be. The better these skills are, the more able you are to take on complex problems and projects with confidence of a successful outcome.

It is likely that many people over-estimate the quality of the critical thinking they bring to activities such as reading, watching television, using the Internet, or to work and study. It is not unusual to assume our point of view is well-founded, that we know best, and that we are logical and reasonable. Other people observing us may not share this view. A lack of self-awareness and weak reasoning skills can result in unsatisfactory appraisals at work or poor marks for academic work. Certainly, comments from lecturers indicate that many students are prevented from gaining better marks because their work lacks evidence of rigorous critical thinking.

All my own work!

Wonky homes! You'll grow to love it! (Really)

Your annual self-appraisal says you have excellent skills in construction, marketing skills and self-presentation. Fortunately for you, my poor critical thinking skills force me to agree.

26 UNIT 2 GAMES

Study skills

STUDY SKILLS Recording achievement

Getting started

Discuss these questions with a partner.

1 Think about the last course or module you passed. What did you do to achieve this?
2 What did you learn about yourself from this experience?
3 How can you use this knowledge to help you in the future?

Scenario

Read about what Kyung-mi has been advised to do in order to further her academic progress. What information would you include in a personal portfolio?

Consider it

Look at these tips on how to record achievement. Do you do any of these things?

1 Write about how you managed to achieve your objectives. For instance, the stages you went through or the personal qualities you used.
2 Include the personal goals you have achieved. For example, becoming more confident in your own ability or finding a study partner.
3 Take notes on what you learned about yourself. For example, what time of day is best for studying, where the best place to study is, or how your level of confidence has changed.
4 Record the ways you kept yourself motivated during the process.
5 Make a list of new skills and qualities you have gained and provide examples of them.
6 Prepare yourself to continue your progress. Make a personal statement of new goals and objectives. State their significance both personally and academically. Continue to update your progress—where you are at the present time, where you want to be, and how you will make progress.

Over to you

Discuss these questions with a partner.

1 What things would you like to try? Why?
2 Discuss one of your achievements using points 1–6. How much does this help you understand your success?
3 What tips would you add to the above list?

Kyung-mi has had a successful first semester academically. She has passed all of her module one exams and is ready to start module two. Her faculty advisor has told her that she must record her achievement and use this knowledge to further her progress.

The faculty advisor has also suggested that she keep a personal portfolio. However, Kyung-mi is not sure how to do this. She has always been a good student and has always passed exams. She puts this down to hard work. She has a record of the units and modules passed, but this does not seem like a personal record.

Her friend has told her that her hard work needs to be defined more clearly and that she should consider goal achievement, personal development, and motivation in order to use this experience to help her in her future academic development. Kyung-mi has also decided to take notes on what she did in order to pass the modules.

56 UNIT 5 SPRAWL

STUDY SKILLS SCENARIOS

Using original material, the end-of-unit study skills task gives students a positive or negative scenario to work through. This provides them with the opportunity for personal performance reflection.

SKILLFUL VERSATILITY Both student and teacher facing, the *Skillful* Digibook can be used for group activities in the classroom, on an interactive whiteboard, or by the student alone for homework and extra practice.

DIGIBOOK TOOLBAR The toolbar that appears on each page allows for easy manipulation of the text. Features such as highlighting and a text tool for commenting allow the teacher to add points as the class goes along, and functions like the zoom and grab tool mean the teacher can focus students' attention on the appropriate sections.

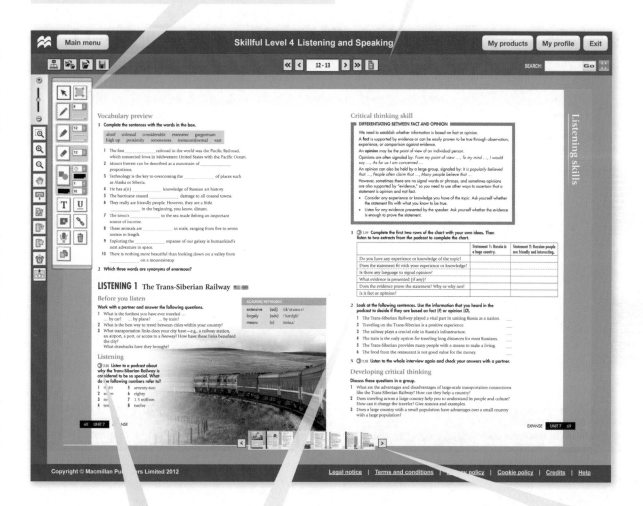

EMBEDDED AUDIO For instant access to the audio for unit exercises, the Digibook has embedded files that you can reach in one click.

PAGE-FAITHFUL Provides a digital replica of the *Skillful* Student's Books while hosting additional, interactive features.

EASY NAVIGATION Jumping from section to section isn't a problem with easy page navigation at both the top and bottom of each page.

WHAT IS *SKILLFUL* PRACTICE? The *Skillful* practice area is a student-facing environment designed to encourage extra preparation, and provides additional activities for listening, vocabulary, grammar, speaking, and pronunciation, as well as support videos for listening and alternative unit assignments.

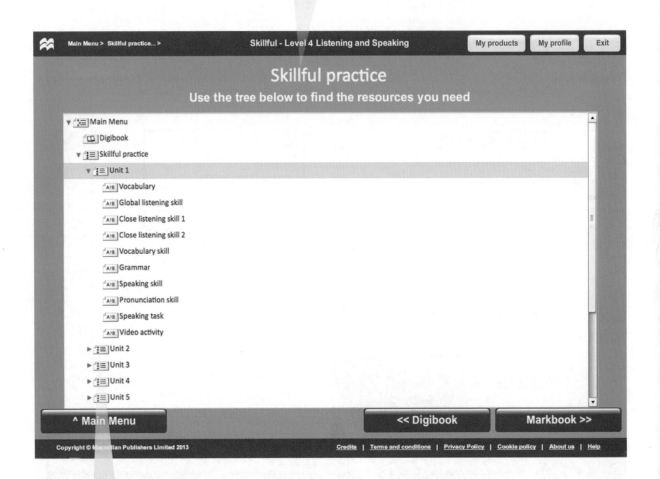

UNIT AND TASK SELECTION
Handy drop-down menus allow students to jump straight to their practice unit and the exercise they want to concentrate on.

ADDITIONAL MATERIAL Along with the student add-ons there are printable worksheets, test materials, and a markbook component to grade and monitor student progress.

TEACHER RESOURCES *Skillful* teachers have many more resources at their fingertips.

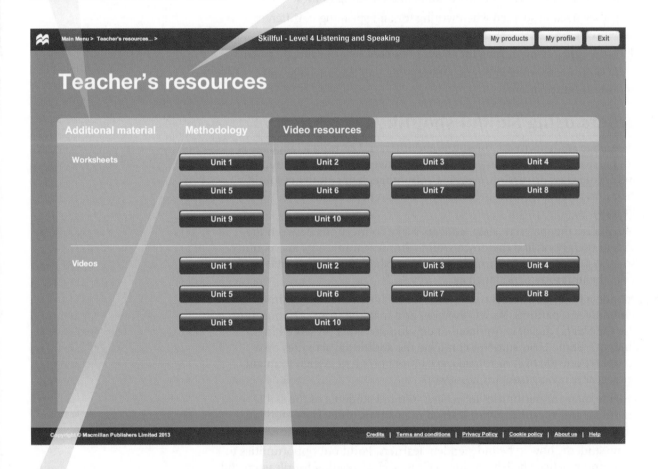

METHODOLOGY For teachers who may need a little extra help to effectively utilize all of the resources *Skillful* has to offer, there are course methodology notes.

VIDEO RESOURCES Teachers have access to the same videos as the students, and to complement these there are printable video worksheets to aid lesson planning.

To the teacher

Academic success requires so much more than memorizing facts. It takes skills. This means that a successful student can both learn and think critically. *Skillful* helps teachers prepare their students for academic work in English by teaching not only language—vocabulary and grammar—but the necessary skills to engage with topics, texts, and discourse with classmates.

Skillful gives students

- engaging texts on a wide variety of topics, each examined from two different academic disciplines
- skills for learning about a wide variety of topics from different angles and from different academic areas
- skills they need to succeed when reading and listening to these texts
- skills they need to succeed when writing for and speaking to different audiences
- skills for critically examining the issues presented by a speaker or a writer
- study skills for learning and remembering the English language and important information.

Teachers using *Skillful* should:

- Encourage students to ask questions and interact. Learning a language is not passive. Many of the tasks and exercises involve pairwork, groupwork, and whole-class discussion. Working with others helps students solidify their understanding, and challenge and expand their ability to think critically.

- Personalize the material. Help students make connections between the texts in their book and their own world—home, community, and country. Bring in outside material from local sources when it's relevant, making sure it fits the unit topics and language.

- Provide a lot of practice. Have students do each exercise several times, with different partners. Review exercises and material from previous units. Use the *Skillful* digital component to develop the skills presented in the Student's Book. Have students complete the additional activities on a computer outside of class to make even more progress. Assign frequent manageable review tasks for homework.

- Provide many opportunities for review. Remind students of the skills, grammar, and vocabulary they learned in previous units. Have students study a little bit each day, not just before tests.

- Show students how to be independent learners. Point out opportunities to study and practice English outside of class, such as reading for pleasure and using the Internet in English. Have them find and share information about the different unit topics with the class. The *Study skills* section in every unit gives students valuable tips for successfully managing their own learning.

Learning skills, like learning a language, takes time and practice. Students must be patient with themselves as they put in the necessary time and effort. They should set and check goals. Periodic assessments the teacher can print, such as the unit tests, progress tests, and end test on the digital component let students see their own progress and measure how much they've learned, so they can feel proud of their academic and linguistic development.

The *Skillful* blend by Dorothy E. Zemach

In some academic disciplines, students can begin by acquiring a lot of facts and general knowledge. In a language, however, students need far more than information—they need skills. They need to know how to do things: how to explain, persuade, ask for help, extend an invitation, outline and argue a thesis, distinguish between important and unimportant information, follow digressions, understand implied information, and more.

Skillful recognizes that skills such as these can't be learned by memorizing facts. To acquire these skills, students must notice them as they read or listen; break them down and understand them through clear explanations; and then rehearse and apply those skills in carefully scaffolded activities that lead to freer practice.

The listening and reading texts in each unit introduce students to one subject area explored through two different academic disciplines and two distinct genres. Students learn and practice both global skills, such as recognizing tone and identifying the main idea, and close skills, such as understanding pronoun references and figuring out vocabulary from context, to understand the texts on several levels.

These days, students must interact with both digital and printed text, online and offline, in the classroom and in the workplace. The *Skillful* textbooks are therefore supplemented with the *Skillful* digital components. These further develop, explain, and extend the skills work found in the printed textbooks. They provide additional exercises related to the skills, the grammar points, and the vocabulary areas. They can be accessed either via the Digibook or through the *Skillful* practice area. Scores are tracked and recorded, and if students work offline, their markbook will be updated the next time they connect to the Internet.

Videos for each unit provide additional subject area content that review the skills and language taught in the unit. The videos can be shown in class to feed in additional content, and the accompanying worksheets can be used to structure the lesson.

Unit checklists help students keep track of language in the unit and review for tests.

The digital components also help teachers with classroom organization and management by assigning and tracking homework, and monitoring student progress using the markbook. A full suite of test materials can be used for placement into the appropriate level, and then provide end-of-unit tests and end-of-course tests that can be used as both formative assessments (to evaluate progress) and summative assessments (to mark achievements and assign grades). Tests are provided in both editable and non-editable formats enabling teachers to manipulate the content, as desired. The format of these tests is similar to internationally recognized standardized tests.

Dorothy E. Zemach taught ESL for over 18 years, in Asia, Africa, and the U.S. She holds an MA in TESL, and now concentrates on writing and editing ELT materials and conducting teacher training workshops. Her areas of specialty and interest are teaching writing, teaching reading, business English, academic English, and testing.

Teaching study skills by Stella Cottrell

There is a growing awareness that students' performance, even in higher education, can be improved through training in relevant academic skills.

Hurley (1994) described study skills as "key skills for all areas of education, including advanced study" and argued that students benefit when these skills are taught explicitly. In other words, it should not be assumed that the skills a student brings from school, or even from the first year of university, are sufficient to carry them through their degree. Skills such as task management, working with others, and critical thinking need to be fine-tuned and extended as students move from one level to another.

Globally, universities and colleges are giving far more attention to preparatory support for prospective students and to developing study skills once a student is on a program. In some countries, there is a growing emphasis, too, on "employability skills," from soft skills such as communication, creativity, and working collaboratively to new attributes sought by employers, including business acumen, cross-cultural sensitivity, and enterprise. In addition, each institution tends to identify a range of skills and qualities that it wants to see embodied by its graduates.

One of the challenges is articulating what is meant by study skills in this changing environment. This has significance for students when trying to make sense of long lists of skills that they are expected to accumulate during their time in higher education. It also has a bearing on who teaches and supports study skills. In some colleges and universities, this falls to study skills specialists; in others, it may be allocated to teaching staff. In each case, different approaches are used to make sense of the learning experience.

From the students' perspective, it helps to organize study skills into a few, relatively easy-to-remember categories. In the latest version of *The Study Skills Handbook*, I suggest using four basic categories:

1 Self   2 Academic   3 People   4 Task

The starting place for students is being able to manage themselves within a new learning environment with confidence and resilience. They need to understand the rationale for, and benefits of, independent study and the kinds of challenges that they will be set. This involves organizing their time, coping with deadlines, and recognizing what it means to take charge of their own learning. It also includes metacognitive skills in reflecting on how they think, learn, and manage themselves for study.

Academic skills consist of such skills as the core research skills (finding, recording, and using information); thinking skills (critical thinking skills, creative problem-solving, and synthesis); understanding academic conventions (the nature and integrity of academic study); and writing skills.

People skills are increasingly important as collaborative study becomes a feature of higher education. These include such skills as giving and receiving criticism, supporting others without cheating, group project work, and playing an active role in group sessions. These can be an especial challenge for international students who may be used to different kinds of learning interactions.

Task management skills within this learning context include such skills as meeting given requirements, and using appropriate protocols and project management in order to achieve a given academic task such as writing an essay or report, undertaking research, conducting an experiment, or solving a problem.

An additional value of this framework is that the basic shell can be easily adapted to other contexts, such as employability. The "Self / People / Tasks" model is one that I used, for example, within *Skills for Success: Personal Development and Employability* (2010).

Stella Cottrell is Director for Lifelong Learning at the University of Leeds, U.K. She is author of the bestselling *The Study Skills Handbook, The Palgrave Student Planner, The Exam Skills Handbook, Critical Thinking Skills, Study Skills Connected,* and *Skills for Success,* all published by Palgrave Macmillan.

Reference
Hurley, J. (1994), *Supporting Learning* (Bristol: The Staff College and Learning Partners).

Teaching vocabulary by Stacey H. Hughes

Teaching vocabulary is more than just presenting words and asking students to learn them. Many students rely on translating words because they lack the strategies which lead to deeper learning of vocabulary. Especially at higher levels, where vocabulary is more abstract, students need to learn vocabulary skills. This essay will look at strategies for introducing, recording, and recalling vocabulary.

Introducing vocabulary

Vocabulary can be introduced in or out of context. Out of context, students must rely on translators, dictionaries, or the teacher for the meaning. Translators are not ideal for real vocabulary learning because it is difficult for students and teachers to assess the translation choice for the context. Encouraging students to use a good monolingual learner's dictionary to find the meaning of words builds dictionary skills and learner autonomy. Online versions are also useful for students looking for a quick definition while online, and they also provide American and British pronunciations. For vocabulary introduced in context, students have to decipher the meaning of the word within the sentence or paragraph without reference to outside sources. They need training in looking for lexical clues in the text around the word and in deciphering meaning through inference. These will have a positive impact on their reading speed and comprehension.

What do students need to know about new words? First is meaning, register, and connotation. If there are several meanings, the one that fits the context best is important. Second is how the word is used, including word forms which help students use words more flexibly, and collocation to avoid sounding "awkward"—increasingly important as students gain proficiency at higher levels. Finally is spelling and pronunciation. Pronunciation is important even in a reading and writing class because words will inevitably come up in other contexts.

Recording vocabulary

Vocabulary notebooks are an excellent tool for students. The very act of noting down new words in a systematic, context-rich way is an important part of the learning cycle. A detailed vocabulary notebook will also be useful for further study. To this aim, students should note down information about words and phrases that will enable them to remember the meaning, and use them later.

Recalling vocabulary

To process meaning and usage more deeply, students should write their own sentences with the words. This active experimentation further reinforces the learning and makes vocabulary more memorable. The goal is to help students move from recognition of the word to feeling more confident using it. One way you can do this is to ask students to review new words at home within 24 hours in order to move them from short-term to long-term memory.

It is also helpful to build in vocabulary revision activities into each lesson. A useful resource for this is a class vocabulary box. Students write the vocabulary from the units onto separate cards, noting information they feel is useful and writing a sentence. Words can then be drawn from the box in vocabulary revision activities or used for independent review. Revision can take many forms, including class competitions, quick spelling "quizzes," or students testing each other. A final benefit of class review is that it teaches students revision skills that they can then incorporate into their own learning strategies.

Students may not have effective vocabulary learning strategies, so teaching them ways to handle, record, and revise new words will make a huge difference to students' vocabulary repertoire.

Stacey H. Hughes is a lecturer at Oxford Brookes University. Her main interests in ELT are learner engagement, active learning, critical thinking, and intercultural issues.

How specific should ESP be? by Louis Rogers

Many argue that English for General Academic Purposes (EGAP) is not specific enough and that courses should be tailored to teach English for Specific Academic Purposes (ESAP). The question is, though, how far can we practically and feasibly be specific? Also should specificity or transferability be prioritized?

For EGAP One basic argument is that it might be too challenging for both teachers and students to fully engage in ESAP. The specific subject knowledge may make the teacher feel deskilled, and arguably students lack sufficient proficiency to deal with the specificity. Additionally, many believe there are generic transferable skills useful across a range of disciplines, and that there is a common core language. Moving from a pedagogic perspective to a practical one brings in other issues. Few institutions would have the resources, time, or facilities to run EAP courses for all their degrees.

For ESAP In support of ESAP, Hyland (2006) presents a number of other arguments. Firstly, subject degree tutors have limited time, inclination, or expertise to teach discipline-specific features, meaning they need to be taught in the EAP classroom. However, the main argument is that we do not know clearly enough what the core transferable language and skills features are. Research also indicates that a greater level of specificity increases engagement and motivation.

Vocabulary Since the development of the Academic Word List by Averil Coxhead there has been a much greater focus on what vocabulary should be taught in EAP. Vocabulary is also one of the main areas proponents for ESAP highlight in their discussions. Hyland and Tse (2007) raise a number of concerns with using general lists, for example, which word is academic: *quantitative* or *qualitative*? Do words such as *attribute* and *volume* have the same meaning across disciplines? One of their main recommendations is to use subject-specific corpora rather than general ones. However, as Eldridge (2008) argues, there are challenges and possibly flaws in this approach. Subjects are not necessarily very specific, and can be quite broad and interdisciplinary in reality. Understandably, research continues in this area, and lists such as the Academic Keywords List have been created (Paquot, 2010).

How specific is any one course? Searching the word *Business* on the Universities and Colleges Admissions System (UCAS) in the U.K. finds over 3,000 courses. A search for *Accountancy* brings up near 700 courses which combine Accountancy with subjects from Management to Divinity, and IT to Psychology. Of course, this only considers the degree name and not individual modules. Some degrees can appear quite similar, but at a modular level they can be diverse. America could be said to be even more interdisciplinary. Students take modules from across the university with some making it compulsory for a Social Science student to take a Science module and vice versa. Furthermore, many universities' mission statements include the word "interdisciplinary." Cambridge University, for example, sees the interdisciplinary nature of the colleges as a major stimulus to teaching and learning. If a university values, at its core, cross-curricular learning, then this clearly impacts on the arguments for ESAP. When these arguments don't negate the possible need for and importance of ESAP, in a multidisciplinary context how specific should we be? Arguably, it is not an either/or situation. ESAP is not the pinnacle to aspire to, and EGAP is not so generic to be derided. Both have their place, but any ESAP course should consider the interdisciplinary nature of academia.

Coxhead, A. (2000). A New Academic Word List. TESOL Quarterly, Vol. 34, 213–238

Eldridge, J (2008). "No, There Isn't an 'Academic Vocabulary,' But …" TESOL Quarterly, 42, 109–113(5)

Hyland, K and Tse, P. (2007). Is there an "academic vocabulary"? TESOL Quarterly, 41, 235–253.

Paquot, M. (2010). *Academic Vocabulary in Learner Writing: From Extraction to Analysis.* New York: Continuum.

Louis Rogers has been an English language teacher for over ten years, working in the U.K., Germany, Portugal, and Italy. His particular professional interests are the use of corpora in developing teaching materials and in breaking down the barriers between EFL fields to make the transition easy for both students and teachers.

Teaching listening skills by Lida Baker

These days, most listening lessons adhere to a three-stage teaching sequence that includes pre-listening, while-listening, and post-listening activities. Within this framework, the primary functions of the listening teacher are:

- to guide students through the listening activities in the textbook;
- to assess at each stage whether or not students are "getting it";
- to take corrective measures if students are struggling.

The following tips can enhance your learners' listening ability.

1 Do not skip the pre-listening stage.

This may seem obvious, but many teachers skip the pre-listening activities "to save time." These teachers miss the point. Pre-listening activities call up students' prior knowledge, and pre-teach language and information that students will need in order to complete the listening activities. By skipping this stage, students are deprived of learning opportunities and their chances of succeeding in the listening tasks are reduced.

2 Make sure students have a clear purpose for listening.

Students will be more motivated to listen if they have a *purpose* for the listening they are about to do. Use generic questions to fix this purpose, such as "What do you think you will learn from this listening text?" or "What questions do you hope this listening text will answer?"

3 Observe as students listen.

While students are listening, observe how well they are performing the while listening task. Watch for students who appear to be having difficulty. Likewise, notice which parts of the task are hard for many students to do.

4 If students are struggling, stop the recording and take corrective measures.

Such measures include micro-lessons and skill modeling. A micro-lesson can be as simple as defining a key vocabulary item, giving necessary background information, or doing a quick minimal-pair drill to enable students to hear the difference between two sounds. Skill modeling is helpful if you see that students are having difficulty performing a complex task such as taking notes in outline form. To model a skill, replay part of the recording and model the skill. Then play another small section and ask students to try it. Both of these contribute crucially to students' acquisition of English, since information that is provided at the point of necessity has a greater likelihood of being retained.

5 Do not "give" students the answers to comprehension questions.

When reviewing comprehension questions, ask students which answers they wrote, and ask them why they chose those particular answers. To guide their responses, ask questions such as: "Which words or facts helped you choose that answer?" Questions like these help students develop their listening strategies and provide you with valuable clues regarding their listening processes. If significant numbers of students missed a question, consider replaying the relevant part of the audio and giving them a chance to try again.

6 Recognize the value of students' errors.

Wrong answers may be a result of extraneous factors (the student is sleepy, the room is too warm, etc.), but more often they are a consequence of gaps in students' knowledge of vocabulary, grammar, and so on. Errors help you identify these gaps and decide what to do or what to teach next.

In conclusion, as we work through listening lessons with students, we should keep in mind that the purpose of teaching is not to "get through the lesson" or even to note the percentage of questions students are able to answer correctly. Getting the right answers is almost incidental to what should be our goal: To help students improve their listening skills and facilitate their acquisition of English.

Lida Baker has been involved in ESL for more than 30 years. She is one of the authors of *Skillful* Listening & Speaking Level 1 and has written several exercise books, teacher's manuals, test packages, and online courses, and is a lifelong member of TESOL and Past Chair of the Materials Writers Interest Section.

UNIT 1 GATHERING

Critical thinking	Inferring a speaker's attitude
	Applying a theory to other situations
Language development	Binomials
	Modal verbs and levels of directness
Pronunciation	Intonation and attitude
Speaking	Interrupting

As this is the first lesson, it is worth spending some time making sure that students feel relaxed and comfortable. Ask students if they know what the unit title, *Gathering*, means. Ask for some examples of gatherings and write them on the board (e.g., a family party or a sports event).

Make sure students understand that a gathering is a group of people coming together. Ask students to look at the picture on page 7 and say what they think it portrays. Ask questions to stimulate ideas: *What can you see in the picture? What do you think may be happening or has happened? How do you think the picture is related to the unit title, Gathering?* etc.

Remember that at any stage, either in- or out of class, the students can access the *Skillful* digital component through the access codes in their Student's Books. Teachers can also access extra items such as tests through the access codes in the Teacher's Book. The activities in the digital component don't have to be done in a fixed order. In the digital component, both students and teachers can also find the Digibook. This is a page-faithful representation of the Student's Book. It could be used to project onto a screen such as an interactive whiteboard.

Discussion point

Ask the students to look at the first question and to complete the task on their own before comparing with a partner. Write any other groups that students think of on the board.

Give students time to discuss questions 2 and 3 with a partner. Afterwards, find out who in the group prefers to be a leader, and who prefers to watch and listen. Ask students what other typical roles or behavior you might find in a group. You could expand the discussion in question 3 to talk about the different roles and behavior people have in these groups.

Vocabulary preview

Cultural awareness

In certain cultures and educational settings, it can be common for the students to lead a seminar, but in others this can be an alien concept. If you are in a multilingual classroom, find out who has led a seminar before. Some people might feel uncomfortable leading a seminar as they see this as the role of the teacher. Keep this in mind when setting up any activity as it could affect how well the task works.

Ask students to work in groups and write definitions of a *seminar*, a *lecture*, and a *meeting*. Next, ask students to think of the different roles and expectations of students and lecturers in seminars and lectures, and get feedback from the class. Then ask students to complete the information with the words in the box.

ANSWERS
1 professor
2 coordinator
3 handouts
4 nominated
5 participation
6 objectives
7 figure out
8 chaotic

LISTENING 1 Three meetings

Before you listen

Some of these words might be new to the students. Ask them to discuss the possible differences between the pairs of words without looking at a dictionary if possible. Then get feedback as a class.

POSSIBLE ANSWERS
1 A **lecture** is a type of formal presentation that might have one key speaker and is not interactive. It could involve technological support. A **seminar** is a more interactive, less formal discussion in which speakers share ideas on a topic.
2 A **summit** is often a formal political conference in which a high-level topic is presented and discussed among key representatives. A **rally** can also be political, but the participants are typically citizens who are protesting about a government or corporate proposal. A rally is often held outdoors, so it does not usually utilize technology, although it could be recorded and broadcast on the Internet.
3 An **audio conference** is either Internet- or telephone-based. It is a formal meeting, often in a business setting, to present a proposal or plan. Most of the participants are connected remotely. A **webinar**

also has people connected remotely on the Internet. There is usually one key speaker presenting on a topic, although there are opportunities for the listeners to interact.

4 A **get-together** is a kind of informal gathering, often among friends who might want to catch up after not seeing each other for a while. They might have the get-together at someone's house or at a public venue, such as a restaurant. An **interview** is a more formal gathering of people, often in the context of one person being interviewed for a job. The format of the interview might be pre-determined. An interview could either be conducted face-to-face or remotely, online.

Listening

1   Make sure students understand what they are listening for. Ask students to discuss with a partner how they might be able to identify which type of interaction is taking place. If students are struggling, give examples: *How many speakers are there? How formal is it? Are they referring to any technology?* Then play the audio.

AUDIO SCRIPT 1.02
Meeting 1

Professor: Good afternoon, everyone. Yes, good afternoon.

Class: Good afternoon.

Professor: Thank you, and welcome to Sociology 101. My name is Professor Chiu. It's very nice to meet you all. Can you all … umm … can you all hear me well? Yes? Even at the back? Good. So, welcome again to Sociology 101. This course will introduce you to the study of one of the most important aspects of the human race—the social group. If you think about it, everything that we do is influenced by the society in which we live. All our achievements are the product of human groups, of gatherings of people together. The aims and objectives of this course are … That sounds like someone's phone ringing. Or it's a text message … or an email. I forgot to say before, there are some dos and don'ts in this class. Phones making noises count as a "don't," So, can I ask everyone to please turn off their phones or put them in silent mode? I guess I'd better do the same. … Yes. Yes. … Where were we? Yes, the aims and objectives of the course. In Sociology 101, we will examine the various skills and techniques sociologists use when they are studying groups of people. We will also examine a wide variety of groups and the behaviors that characterize them.

Meeting 2

Woman 1: Hello, everyone. Are we all ready to get this meeting started? … Well. This term we've been given a project that we have to do as a team. Professor Baker nominated me as the group leader so … Now, sooner or later we need to figure out how we're going to work on this. I thought we could start now.

Woman 2: When is the project due?

Woman 1: The information is on the first page of the handout that the professor gave us.

Woman 2: What handout? I don't have the handout.

Woman 1: OK. Does anyone have an extra handout for … sorry what's your name?

Woman 2: Susan.

Woman 3: Yes. Here you are.

Woman 2: Thanks very much. Sorry about that. I wasn't in the class when we were given the handouts for this project.

Woman 1: That's OK.

Woman 2: And I had to call a friend to find out which group I was in, and she told me …

Woman 1: OK. So first we need to decide how …

Woman 4: I'm sorry, I think I'm in the wrong group. I can't see my name on the list.

Woman 1: Oh. OK.

Woman 4: Sorry, I'll just leave now. Excuse me. Excuse me.

Woman 1: So. Are we ready to start? Does everyone have the handout?

All: Yes.

Woman 1: Everyone in the right group?

All: Yes.

Woman 1: So. How do we want to start this project? I mean, should we divide it into sections? … There are six of us, so I think the work might go quicker if we divide it into three sections and two people take a section each.

Woman 2: How about two of us do the initial research, two of us interview some professors, and the other two put the PowerPoint together?

Woman 3: Maybe we can have a fourth group write the script for the whole project when we present it.

Woman 1: Exactly. Although perhaps we can all write the script together. Do you think we need a coordinator? Someone who can take minutes and distribute meeting information to the group?

All: Sure. OK. Mmm.

Woman 4: You should be the coordinator!

Woman 1: I don't mind. What … what do other people think?

All: OK. Whatever. Sure.

Woman 1: Right, so I will coordinate the project. Who wants to do the initial research?

Meeting 3

Man 1: Gentlemen, let's get started. Wow. It's good to see so many new faces. We have been going strong now for over 80 years on campus, and it's really only because we get so many new members arriving every year. It's really great to be part of something with so much history. I think all our former members will agree that being in the university debating society is a great way to integrate into campus life, make new friends, and meet other people with similar interests. But not only that, it's also great for your future. Taking an active role here really can help your speaking and presentation skills, help you to think critically and analytically, and build your résumé. First of all is that, as members, you can ask me, or one of the other people up here, anything you need to know about the debating society. We have an "open door" policy, so we encourage you to drop by anytime.

Man 2: Excuse me?

Man 1: Yes?

Man 2: Can I ask a question now?

Man 1: Sure, go ahead.

Man 2: You have an office? I don't know where the office is.

Man 1: I was just getting to that. It's on the third floor of Smith Hall. Room 305. We share it with the chess club and the accountants' association. Actually, if everyone can just wait for the end of the meeting for questions. We've got a lot to tell you, and maybe your questions will be answered.

Man 2: OK.

Man 1: Great. Let's get started then. What have I talked about? Ummm … getting involved. Check. Open door policy. Check. Next … oh yeah. The most important thing! Our first debate is next week!

Man 3: What is the topic?

Man 4: What day is it?

Man 5: Will there be time to practise?

Man 6: How do you choose the teams?

Man 1: Please everyone. PLEASE. Just wait until the end of the meeting before asking the questions. We have a LOT to explain! So … as I was saying …

POSSIBLE ANSWERS
Meeting 1—a lecture
The purpose is for a professor to give students an overview of the Sociology 101 course. We can assume that this is the first meeting between the professor and the students, and that the students are not fully aware of the lecture protocols. The interaction level is fairly formal, with the professor leading the meeting.

Meeting 2—a seminar (or a semi-formal, academic get-together)
This meeting occurs in an academic setting in a classroom or similar interior space. There is a lead speaker who monitors the pattern of discussion. The purpose is to set up a group project, delegating roles to the participants.

Meeting 3—a seminar (or a semi-formal, academic get-together)
This meeting appears to be the initial meeting for students new to a university debating society. The

speaker introduces the purpose of the debating society and formally covers a list of points.

2   Before playing the audio again, ask students to discuss how they identified what type of gathering each one was. Try to extract references to specific examples from the audio. Once you have done this, play the audio again and ask them to answer the questions.

POSSIBLE ANSWERS
1   Sociology
2   one don't—phones making noises
3   One woman queries the project due date. One woman doesn't have a handout. One woman is in the wrong group and leaves.
4   She suggests dividing the work into three sections and that two people take a section each.
5   It's a great way to integrate into campus life, make new friends, and meet other people with similar interests. In addition, taking an active role in the debating society can help your speaking and presentation skills, help you think critically and analytically, and build your résumé.
6   an open door policy

Critical thinking skill

Write *attitude* on the board and elicit a definition from students. If students are unclear, explain that it is related to how someone feels about something. Then read the following sentences aloud to students. Use your intonation to show the emotion in parentheses.

What happened? (concerned)
What happened? (angry)

Ask students how they would describe your attitude and emotion each time. Then ask them to read the *Inferring a speaker's attitude* box.

1   Check that students understand the meaning of the adjectives in 1–3. You could get the students to say a short sentence using the intonation of the adjectives to prepare for the listening. Then play the audio and ask students to do the exercise.

ANSWERS
1 c   2 b   3 b

2   When checking the answers, you could project the audio script onto the screen or provide copies. Students can then highlight words that showed the speaker's attitude or places where they thought the intonation demonstrated the speaker's attitude. You might want to play the audio again to highlight the use of intonation.

Developing critical thinking

These questions do not specifically develop the skill in the previous section, but rather they get students to think critically about the content of the discussions they have just heard. To reinforce the critical thinking skill of inferring a speaker's attitude, you could ask students to discuss the questions once. After this, put students into new groups and explain that the aim this time is to practice the use of intonation to emphasize their attitude. Students should take turns to state their answer to one of the questions and should try to use different intonation patterns to convey their attitude. If students are struggling, this could be done as a role play. You could prepare cards with opinions and attitudes on them, and students could role-play the discussion. Once students have done this, ask one or two to demonstrate their answer, and drill as necessary to emphasize the attitude of the speaker.

LISTENING 2 Getting from *you and me*, to *we*

Before you listen

Cultural awareness

The ideas in this section are based on an individualistic culture. In some cultures, the idea of "we" is very much at the heart of the culture. To a collectivist culture, where the group is more important than the individual, the ideas presented here might seem a little strange. Western Europe and the United States are typically individualistic cultures, whereas countries such as China, Korea, and Japan tend to be more collectivist. You might want to find out the dominant approach for any nationalities in your class as this could lead to an interesting pre-listening discussion.

1 Ask students to explain the meaning of the expression. Then ask them to discuss any similar expressions students have in their own language.

POSSIBLE ANSWER
It means that the bigger picture, or the final outcome, carries more weight or is more important than the parts that made it.

2 Put students into pairs to do the task. Then write *successful* and *unsuccessful* at the top of the board. Write up any ideas students have for what makes a group successful or unsuccessful.

Listening

1 Remind students of the different kinds of meetings from *Listening 1* and then play the audio.

AUDIO SCRIPT 1.03

Professor: So, are we ready? Our first topic is group dynamics in the online environment. Does anyone want to start us off? … Well, you've all come across Bruce Tuckman's work on group dynamics theory? Yes? If you remember, he talks about stages of group formation. Can anyone remember what these are?

Sam: I can.

Professor: Go ahead.

Sam: Tuckman's theory tells us that when a group forms, it goes through several distinctive stages. These are forming, storming, norming, performing, and closing.

Jane: I read adjourning. Forming, storming, norming, performing, and adjourning.

Sam: I think closing is like adjourning. Anyway, there were five stages.

Professor: So. Forming, storming, norming, performing, and adjourning. Now, this theory was written in 1965. Before the Internet came into our lives. The question is, do people form groups in the same way online? Let's go through Tuckman's stages one by one to make sure we're all on the same page. Stage one is forming. What happens?

Rachael: In this stage, the members of the group first come together.

Professor: Exactly. Now, can you think of examples where online groups might form, even though the members are distributed?

Sam: Online game communities?

Jane: Groups of bloggers communicating? Or groups within social media?

Rachael: People working on a wiki?

Sam: I read that in this stage, the forming stage, it's important that there is clear leadership and direction from the team leader.

Professor: Yes, and that's of particular relevance to the area of online education, where there needs to be a skilled facilitator. So what about stage two?

Jane: Stage two is storming. Individual members may begin to voice their differences. There may be splits of opinion, or disagreements as to how the group should work.

Professor: Right, and depending on cultural factors, this may result in open conflict within the group. You could say this is a make or break stage. For some groups, they never get past stage two, they break up as a group there—but once the storm has passed, the group moves into stage three, norming. Sam?

Sam: This is when the group agrees on how to behave and how their goals can be achieved.

Jane: A bit like the calm after the storm.

Sam: The members of the group understand each other and can move forward.

Professor: And then? Stage four?

Rachael: Performing. I have it here. In this stage, the team is working effectively and efficiently towards a goal. It is during this stage that the team leader can take more of a back seat. Individual members take more responsibility in the group process, and their participation is stronger. The group's energy is strong, and it can achieve a lot during this stage.

Professor: And finally stage five?

Jane: Is the last one, closing or adjourning. It's about closing and moving on, this stage.

Professor: So, those are the stages, but the question is, do groups online go through the same stages?

Rachael: I think so, yes. In fact, according to Forsyth in his ... just a second, OK yes, here it is. According to Forsyth in his 2009 text *Group Dynamics*, members in online groups are as likely to conform to group behaviour as those in face-to-face groups.

Professor: Yes, exactly. And this is what's interesting, given that originally many experts thought that online groups would be chaotic and unstructured since nobody could really see each other. And of course, it's interesting to note that—in the area of online education—online classes, when moderated by a teacher successfully, reproduce many of the stages of group dynamics that Tuckman outlined.

ANSWERS
1 a seminar (or academic discussion group)
2 The speakers consist of a professor, who is leading the topic, and students, who are making contributions to the topic.
3 Group dynamics is about the way speakers interact in a group. *physics gymnastics mathematics politics*

2 Ask students to discuss the question in pairs and feed back to the class. Ask them to explain why they chose their answer and why the others are incorrect.

ANSWER
b

Critical thinking skill

Ask students to read the information in the *Applying a theory to other situations* box. Explain any unknown words and check understanding by asking: *Why is a theory useful? How can we show we understand a theory?* etc.

1 Before playing the audio again, ask students to explain any of the terms in the box they can remember to a partner. After listening, students should compare their answers, then feed back as a class.

ANSWERS
1 forming
2 storming
3 performing
4 storming
5 norming
6 norming
7 performing
8 adjourning

2 Set the task in the book. If you have a particularly strong group, you could ask them to write another example such as these. They should then read out their example to the class, who can guess what stage is being exemplified.

ANSWERS
1 performing
2 norming
3 forming
4 performing

Developing critical thinking

1 Once students have discussed the questions in groups, open this up for a class discussion.

2 Considering a range of perspectives will make both students' participation in seminars and their writing more balanced. Ask students to discuss the questions in groups followed by whole-class feedback.

This is a good place to use the video resource *No man is an island*. It is located in the Video resources section of the digital component.

Language development: Binomials

1 Write the following sentence on the board: *The thing to do, foremost and first, is arrange an appropriate meeting venue.*

Ask students what is wrong with this sentence. Elicit the idea of binomials. Tell students to read the *Binomials* box and to complete exercise 1.

ANSWERS
all or nothing	pure and simple
cut and dried	show and tell
give or take	time and effort
loud and clear	ups and downs

2 Set the task in the book and check as a whole class. To extend the task, ask students to write sentences using three of the binomials.

ANSWERS
1 time and effort
2 show and tell
3 loud and clear
4 all or nothing
5 ups and downs
6 cut and dried
7 pure and simple
8 give or take

Language development: Modal verbs and levels of directness

1 Write the following statement onto the board: *We must go to the library to do our research.* Ask students to rewrite the sentence so that it's a suggestion, a request, and an indirect statement. Once they have done this, ask the students to compare their sentences with the ones in the *Modal verbs and levels of directness* box. Then ask students to do the exercise.

POSSIBLE ANSWERS
1 4 2 5 3 2 4 2 5 5 6 4 7 4 8 5

2 Discuss this question as a whole class.

> **POSSIBLE ANSWERS**
> **1** an interview
> **2** friends at home accessing the Internet
> **3** two friends studying together at a library
> **4** a seminar
> **5** a classroom
> **6** a private meeting
> **7** a lecture
> **8** a union rally

3 Students can make the sentences either more or less direct. A number of alternatives are possible. Write one example for each onto the board and check to see if other students have anything particularly different.

4 Ask students to work individually first and then compare their answers with a partner.

SPEAKING Planning a study group

Pronunciation skill

Cultural awareness

The use of pitch and intonation can vary between languages. In English, intonation is frequently used to convey meaning. However, in Mandarin Chinese, pitch helps distinguish words with the same vowels and consonants. Understanding some of these differences can help make learners better speakers and listeners of a language.

1 Ask students to read the *Intonation and attitude* box. Play the audio once and ask students to match a speaker with an attitude. Then play the audio again and ask the students to mark the words where the intonation changes to show a different attitude.

> **AUDIO SCRIPT 1.04**
> **1**
> **A:** I'm sorry, but I can't come to the meeting today.
> **B:** Oh, OK. We'll have the meeting next week then.
> **2**
> **A:** I'm sorry, but I can't come to the meeting today.
> **B:** Oh, OK. We'll have the meeting next week then.
> **3**
> **A:** I'm sorry, but I can't come to the meeting today.
> **B:** Oh, OK. We'll have the meeting next week then.

> **ANSWERS**
> **1 A:** worry   **B:** suspicion
> **2 A:** surprise   **B:** indifference
> **3 A:** anger   **B:** sarcasm

2 After you have played the audio again and students have practiced the dialogues, ask them to write another sentence to demonstrate the different emotions. Each student should say their sentence and their partner should try to guess their emotion. Remind students that sarcasm involves heavy intonation on key words. If they are angry, they should speak quickly, possibly with a raised voice. The intonation to convey suspicion and worry will be similar, but students can make use of body language to assist meaning (frowning for suspicion, or a raised eyebrow for worry).

Speaking skill

Cultural awareness

In some cultures, it can be much more common to talk over people without causing any offence. Such cultures can appear quite loud to some people, as everyone appears to be talking at the same time. Ask students how they feel when people talk over them or interrupt them, or whether one approach is more common than the other in their culture.

1 Ask students to complete the phrases individually.

> **ANSWERS**
> **1** Sorry to interrupt, but …
> **2** May I say something here?
> **3** Do you mind if I say something here?

2 Ask students to work with a partner to practice interrupting each other.

SPEAKING TASK

Many teachers encourage students to form a study group to help them at university. Depending on each student's preference and educational background, this might be something they are happy to do and are familiar with, but for others, this can seem a daunting concept. Some students worry that others will take their ideas. Others might be concerned about their language skills in a group.

Brainstorm

After discussing the questions with a partner, have students share ideas together as a whole class.

Plan

1 Ask students to listen and answer the questions.

> **ANSWERS**
> **1** three
> **2** a study hall (next to the cafeteria)
> **3** 90 minutes, once a week

AUDIO SCRIPT 1.05

A: So, shall we get started?

All: Yes, sure, OK.

A: OK, then. So. A study group. First thing to decide is if we have enough people here for a study group, I mean, there are only four of us …

B: Sorry. Three of us. Chris can't do the study group. Right, Chris?

C: Yeah. But I'll stay for this first meeting.

A: Should we try to get another group together with us for this?

B: No, I don't think so. I think three is fine.

D: Me, too.

A: OK. Three people then. What next?

B: What about a meeting place? We can't meet here …

A: I know. It's a little noisy and not very comfortable.

D: Can I say something here?

A: Sure, go ahead.

D: There's a study hall next to the cafeteria. It's almost always empty. Could we meet there?

A: Sounds good to me.

B: Yeah. I've never been there but …

A: So. We should decide how long to meet for, and how often.

D: I read somewhere that you should make the meeting at the same time every week. Like a class. That way we'd take it more seriously.

B: We may as well make it for this time since we're all here. Is this time OK?

D: Works for me.

A: Me, too.

C: Hang on just a minute. I know I'm not going to be in this group, but aren't we supposed to have a seminar at this time every other week?

A: Umm. No. That's on Thursday.

C: Sorry. Forget I said anything.

A: Don't worry about it.

B: So everyone agrees that this time is fine? Every week?

A: How long should we make it?

B: An hour?

D: Two hours?

A: Two hours seems like … too much. At least to start with.

B: Ninety minutes? Compromise?

A: Is that OK with you, Jeff?

D: Fine by me.

A: OK, so I guess all we have left to decide is exactly what we will do when we meet. I actually have a list of dos and don'ts that I got off the Internet. We could use these as a starting point …

2 Play the audio again and ask students to do the exercise with a partner. You might need to project the conversation onto the board in order for students to identify the modals, intonation patterns, and interruptions.

3 If you would like students to set up study groups for your class, tailor this task to that purpose.

Speak and share

You could make the *Speak* task more interactive and competitive by giving groups cards with the words *interrupt, suggest, offer,* and *request*. Each time a student does one of these functions, they take a card. The winning individual is the one to gain most cards.

During this stage, monitor and take language notes. Use the photocopiable *Unit assignment checklist* on page 88 to assess the students' speaking. If you have set the *Share* task up so that they will form study groups for your class, you can tell students that in the following weeks you will be asking for feedback on how their study group is doing. Make sure that you set a regular feedback time to help this work.

STUDY SKILLS Speaking in groups

Getting started

Ask the students to discuss the questions with a partner. Ask them if they agree with the last question or whether they would choose a different skill, and if so, why.

Scenario

Scenarios are often useful as they can present the student with ideas that might mirror their own situations and work as valuable starting points for making connections from external to personal. Ask students to read the scenario.

> **POSSIBLE ANSWER**
> Jemal should build his confidence in speaking in groups. To build confidence, he could start by expressing interest in the other speakers' ideas, using phrases such as "Really? … That sounds good." He could also practice more with one partner outside of class. He could take things that he likes about the way other speakers speak and try to use them next time.

Consider it

Once students have done the task, ask them to add more phrases to the examples for each tip.

Over to you

Ask students to discuss these questions with a partner. Afterwards, ask students to choose their favorite tip to practice in the next week.

Extra research task

Ask students to research other teamwork theories such as the one in *Listening 2* about Tuckman's teamwork theory. Tell students to look for similarities and differences between the theories.

Critical thinking	Identifying key information in an argument
	Selecting information for notes and summaries
Language development	Prepositional verbs
	Phrasal verbs
Pronunciation	Identifying the linking /r/
Speaking	Agreeing and disagreeing—degrees of formality

Discussion point

Background information

Games have always been part of human life, and their existence seems to reflect a basic need for people to interact in a competitive way, using both imagination and logic. The earliest gaming equipment is thought to be dice, which appear to have originated in Asia. Examples of dice have been found in archeological sites in Iran and date back over 3,000 years. Other early games include dominoes and backgammon. Electronic games initially became popular with arcade games in the 1970s. Consoles then appeared in the 1990s, and the rise of computer games has continued.

Direct students' attention to the picture on page 17. Ask students where the people in the picture are and what they are doing (a gaming café where PCs are networked, and people can log on and compete against each other). Ask students if they have ever been to a gaming café and if so, where, what games did they play, and did they enjoy it. Then allow students time to discuss the questions with a partner. Invite volunteers to share their answers and write them on the board. Ask students to note how many of the games they mentioned are electronic, how many are not, and how many can be both (e.g., scrabble, chess).

Vocabulary preview

Ask students to complete the text without a dictionary. Explain that using the context to work out meaning is an important skill to develop. During class feedback, write the word *dopamine* on the board. Ask students if they know what it is. Explain that it is a chemical in the brain that is connected with reward-motivation and that they will hear more about it in the audio.

ANSWERS

1	stimulating	5	Neurologists
2	motivate	6	dopamine
3	likelihood	7	addiction
4	reward	8	ultimatum

LISTENING 1 Video games: Lessons for life

Before you listen

Before students read the statements, start a general discussion by asking whether using video games is good or bad for you. Write their ideas on the board, but don't comment on them at this point. Students can then work individually to decide if the statements are true or false.

Background information

Many people assume that using video games has a negative impact on people as it has been linked to addiction problems, a reduced ability to socialize effectively, increases in violent behavior, and even obesity. Conversely, this listening text focuses on the positive effects of using video games.

Listening

1 Play the audio and ask students to check their answers to the *Before you listen* exercise.

AUDIO SCRIPT 1.06

Professor: Good morning, everyone. First of all I'd like to thank you and your lecturer for inviting me here today as your guest. For those of you who don't know, I'm principally a lecturer at the university's Entertainment Technology Centre, I also design video games, and I wrote a book called *Video Games: Lessons for life.*

That's what I am here to talk to you about today—video games and the lessons they can teach us about life, and in particular, about learning. I believe that by looking at how video games motivate players and also at how we can learn specific skills from them, we can become better students.

First of all, let's look at motivation. Many people enjoy playing video games. In fact, they are extremely addictive. But why? Why do we want to keep on playing? What do video games do to motivate us? The answer is that video games offer us very strong emotional rewards. How do they do this? The answer is that they directly engage the brain. As you may know from your studies this semester, the neurotransmitter connected to learning called dopamine is also associated with reward-seeking behaviour. Dr. Paul Howard-Jones, a professor in neuroscience in education at the University of Bristol, is currently doing research into ways of helping students learn. He pinpoints video games as an area that gives us greater insight into how learning takes place. Scientists have found a strong relationship between how the brain responds to rewards and the likelihood of learning. How does this work? Well, when someone receives a reward, a part of the brain called the nucleus accumbens is activated.

This in turn increases dopamine uptake. But the nucleus accumbens is also activated when we anticipate a reward, and the level of dopamine spikes twice: first at the moment of anticipation, and also at the moment of receiving the reward. So, the level of dopamine is proportional to the amount you desire something.

So, how can understanding the neural processes of the brain's response to gaming—a very rewarding stimulus—help us in learning? Well, because dopamine helps focus our attention, it enhances our potential for learning. As we anticipate a reward, dopamine is released, and the brain is in an optimal learning-ready state. Video games are often structured so that our anticipation of reward is central to how the game is played. Let's look more closely at this area and link this to five specific points of learning that can be fostered by gaming.

The first point is learning to achieve long-term and short-term aims. In order to progress in a typical game, you have to complete a number of small tasks, and you are generally rewarded for each. This in turn helps you get closer to your long-term aim, which is to complete the game. According to technology theorist Tom Chatfield in 2010, this can be translated into the real world of education—as a student you can be taught to organise your work into smaller tasks like complete these five questions, finish this unit of work, collaborate with other people, or attend a certain number of classes per semester. What you learn is that you have to break down your work into smaller pieces that you complete simultaneously. This can be the key to drawing attention to how you can achieve real life long-term goals such as finish secondary school or get a university degree.

The second lesson is what reward for effort can teach us. Neurologist Judy Willis stated in a 2011 study that video games reward player effort with incremental goal progress, not only final results. What Willis suggests here is that every time you succeed in doing something in a game, you get a credit, through points or advancement. Success is rewarded, but often other skills such as persistence, speed, and observation skills win credit, too. For instance, you may gain an extra life for playing a level for a certain amount of time, even though you don't complete the level, or you might get extra points for completing a task quickly. What it teaches us about life is two things: the first is that it's important to try, but also that there are rewards for using different strategies and skills to tackle problems and tasks.

Lesson number three is what we can learn from feedback. As stated in a research paper—Game-based Learning from 2012 by Jessica Trybus, Director of Edutainment at Carnegie Mellon University—in a game we work towards a goal, choosing actions and experiencing consequences along the way. So the research paper makes reference to how gamers learn that there are positive and negative consequences to their actions, and they learn this quite quickly. We have seen how, in a video game, you can get rewards. For example, you may gain an enormous amount of points, which allows you to continue the game comfortably. However, you could easily lose everything. You can lose all of your points or even die with one risky move. This is also true in real life.

This is a very important lesson to take in because no one can learn unless they are able to connect consequences to actions, especially when the consequences are in the distant future, like global warming or the dangers of pollution. Being able to consider a range of possible consequences to an action allows students to think more reflectively and creatively in the classroom.

Our fourth and fifth lessons are not linked to motivation, reward, or video game structure, but are tangible skills which everyone can learn from the gaming experience. The first is enhanced visual attention. According to a study by Green and Bavelier at the University of Rochester, 2003, playing video games enhances our visual skills. Please note that this is distinct from the concept of attention, as in the ability to pay attention in class. What do we mean by visual attention? Well, there is far more visual information available to us than we are capable of processing. Visual attention is a mechanism through which items are selected for further processing while others are left unnoticed. What is compelling about this is that by playing we are actually doing a vital physical exercise because video games help us focus on what we need to see, but also stay aware of what is going on around us. The real-life benefits of enhanced visual attention can be seen in drivers who are able to monitor more objects at once—this ability makes them safer drivers. In an academic context, greater visual attention helps students develop the reading skills of skimming and scanning. Skimming refers to glancing through a text to determine its gist or general theme, while scanning refers to glancing through a text in search of specific information or to determine its suitability for a given purpose. Given the number of texts an average university student has to read during a degree course, it is a great asset to have enhanced visual attention.

The fifth and final lesson from gaming that I'd like to refer to today is creativity—I find this point particularly fascinating. According to Linda Jackson, professor in psychology at Michigan State University, in 2011, children who play video games tend to be more creative. Her study is the first to provide clear evidence that child gamers become more creative in classroom tasks, such as drawing pictures and writing stories. And, significantly, the research showed that gender, and also the kind of video game played, does not have any impact on creativity. Although boys favoured sports games or games with violent content, and girls preferred games that involved interaction with others, regardless of gender or type of game played there was a clear increase in creativity.

As we know, there are also the negative sides to video games, for instance, game addiction. However, that's an area you will deal with in your next lecture. I came here today to give you the positive view of gaming and its educational value. We can see from these five examples, and there are many more, that through video gaming, we can learn techniques for motivation and skills that can be transferred into real-life situations and benefit us in a learning context. Who said that gaming was a mindless activity? Thank you all for coming along.

ANSWERS

1 not given	4 false
2 true	5 true
3 false	6 true

2 Ask students to order the topics. They can then check their answers in pairs before feeding back to the class.

ANSWERS

1 achieving long- and short-term aims
2 reward for effort
3 learning from feedback
4 enhanced visual attention
5 creativity

Critical thinking skill

Ask students to read the information in the *Identifying key information in an argument* box. Highlight the importance of using examples and evidence to support any arguments in an academic context.

1 Ask students to read the sentences. Play the audio again so that students can identify the key points. They can then check their answers in pairs before feeding back to the class.

ANSWER

Points 2, 3, 4, 6, and 7 contain key information.

2 Students can work in pairs to decide on the key points and the supporting sentences. Check answers with the whole class.

ANSWERS

1 K, E, E	2 K, E, E	3 E, E, K

Developing critical thinking

Ask students to work in groups to read the sentence and decide which point in Exercise 2 of the *Critical thinking skill* section it summarizes. Then have them work individually to write summaries for the other points. When the students have finished, ask them to evaluate their summaries in groups.

ANSWER

The sentence summarizes point 2.

LISTENING 2 Game theory

Before you listen

Ask students to fill in the blanks and then check their answers in pairs before feeding back to the class.

ANSWERS

1 mathematical	5 economics
2 losses	6 negotiations
3 decisions	7 diplomacy
4 cooperate	8 engage

Listening

Focus on the *Academic keywords* box. These words all appear in the audio. Check that students understand the meanings and ask them to check in a dictionary if they are unsure. Practice the pronunciation of the words, particularly *cite* and *prove*.

Ask students to read the assignment carefully before playing the audio.

AUDIO SCRIPT 1.07

Student 1: I've chosen the game Rock, Paper, Scissors. Ummm … for this game basically you need two players. I'm sure you know the rules, but I'll explain them again. Each player has to put their hands behind their backs and count to four. On three they have to make a decision and make the form of a rock (a fist), paper (hand open), or scissors (two fingers outstretched). When they count four, both players "throw" their gesture towards each other. You then calculate who wins using these rules. Rock beats scissors. Scissors beats paper. Paper beats rock.

This simple game illustrates the concept of a zero-sum game. The first person to lay the foundations of this game theory was the mathematician John von Neumann in his 1928 paper "The Theory of Parlor Games." In a zero-sum game, one participant's gain is balanced by another's loss. In other words, there is one winner and one loser, always. To explain it mathematically, if you add the gains and subtract the losses, the total is zero because the number of gains is the same as the number of losses. In real life there are, I read anyway, that there are few real zero-sum games. But you could find examples in trade and economics. For example, two companies bidding on one contract. Only one company can win the contract, and the other has to lose.

Student 2: OK, I'm … well I'm going to talk about a situation called the ultimatum. It's a money-sharing situation. In the ultimatum, a sum of money is given to two players to share between them. When the situation begins, the first player makes a proposal as to how the money will be split. If the second player accepts the proposal, they split the money as agreed. But, if the second player refuses the proposal, neither player gets any money.

One real-life example of this could be bilateral trade negotiations between countries. If the negotiation breaks down because the proposal is considered unfair, then both nations lose the benefits of the trading agreement.

This has interesting sociological consequences, as some social scientists say it proves a human being's unwillingness to accept injustice. According to Güth in his 1995 article called "On Ultimatum Bargaining Experiments," there is quite a bit of debate on whether human decision-making is purely driven by monetary incentives, and he clearly states a preference for fairness as one other key factor in the process.

Student 3: The best example of the assurance situation in game theory that I could find was The Stag Hunt. Two individuals go out on a hunt. Each has to individually choose to hunt a stag or hunt a rabbit, and they must choose which animal to hunt without knowing what the other chooses. An individual can get a rabbit by himself, but a rabbit is worth less than a stag. If an individual hunts a stag, he must have the cooperation of his partner in order to succeed.

There are two outcomes to the stag hunt. Either both hunters hunt the stag together, or both hunters hunt rabbits on their own.

I think you could say that this situation is about risk and a test of social cooperation. Both hunters would prefer to hunt a stag, but they can only do this if they work together. If either hunter isn't sure what the other will choose, they will choose the rabbit as a safe option. This scenario was described by the philosopher Jean Jacques Rousseau in his book from 1754, *A Discourse on Inequality.*

I think we could say it has applications in how businesses can cooperate together. This game represents real-life situations in which people or businesses can cooperate together for greater rewards—the stag—but if they don't trust each other, they opt for the less rewarding but more certain choice—the rabbit—and risk less.

ANSWERS

The ultimatum—money-sharing situation
The assurance situation—The Stag Hunt
The anti-coordination situation—the game of chicken
The Prisoner's Dilemma—why people cooperate

Critical thinking skill

Refer students to the information in the *Selecting information for notes and summaries* box. Ask them to look at the given example. Discuss any ideas for making these notes even clearer (e.g., underlining the point/topic/title). Then ask for suggestions on additional abbreviations that could be used, e.g., using numbers rather than words, (*1*, not *one*), using + instead of *and*, omitting words such as *the*.

1 Ask students to read the summaries carefully and decide which of the two concepts they are from before you play the audio again. Students can then check their answers in pairs before feeding back to the class.

ANSWERS

| 1 A | 3 U | 5 A | 7 A | 9 A |
| 2 U | 4 A | 6 U | 8 U | 10 U |

2 Play the audio and ask students to complete the notes. They may not be able to write down all the relevant information while listening, so ask them to compare their answers with a partner and fill in any gaps together. Then check answers with the whole class.

AUDIO SCRIPT 1.08 *death or glory.*

Student 4: I chose the anti-coordination situation. This one was quite easy, as the example most often cited is one I'd heard of before. It's the game of chicken. Two drivers drive towards each other on a collision course. One of the drivers has to swerve to avoid the other, or they will crash. But if one driver swerves and the other does not, the one who swerves is called a chicken, meaning a coward, and is the loser.

So, the principle of the game is that each player prefers not to yield to (or swerve away from) the other, but if they don't yield, they get the worst possible outcome. It's also known as the Hawk–dove game. I was reading Ross Cressman's book *The Stability Concept of Evolutionary Game Theory* from 1992, and he describes the same scenario as a situation in which there is competition for a shared resource and the contestants can choose either resolution or conflict. One real-world application here is in the world of negotiation in international diplomacy, where neither side wants to back down or lose face, but risks total loss if they don't.

Student 5: OK, the Prisoner's Dilemma is the most famous and important of all game theory situations. At least from what I read. Albert W. Tucker formalized the game aspect in his book *Contributions to the Theory of Games* from 1950. The simple scenario to explain this theory is that it's a mathematical explanation of why people cooperate. In this game, two prisoners are both being held by the police for the same crime. They are in different cells, and the police interview each one separately.

Now, each prisoner has a choice. He can remain silent, or confess and tell the police that his partner is guilty. More importantly, each prisoner knows that the other has the same choice.

If both prisoners stay silent, they each get a one-year sentence. If both confess, if they both try to blame the crime on each other, they each get three years in jail. But, and here's the tricky part, if only one confesses and blames the crime on the other, he goes free. But he sends his partner away for five years.

What makes it a real dilemma is that, logically, the best strategy for each prisoner individually is to confess and blame the crime on the other. But it could provide a worse outcome.

I think the real-world application of this is all about cooperating even when something isn't in your best interests.

ANSWERS
The point/topic/title
The anti-coordination situation
The game of chicken / Hawk–dove game
The most important and relevant information, plus examples

The principle of the game is that each player prefers not to yield to the other, but if they don't yield, they get the worst possible outcome.

A situation in which there is competition for a shared resource and the contestants can choose either resolution or conflict.

Real-world application is in the world of negotiation in international diplomacy, where neither side wants to back down or lose face, but risks total loss if they don't.

The source of the information

Ross Cressman, book, *The Stability Concept of Evolutionary Game Theory*, 1992.

The point/topic/title

The Prisoner's Dilemma

A mathematical explanation of why people cooperate.

The most important and relevant information, plus examples

Each prisoner has a choice. He can remain silent, or confess and tell the police his partner is guilty—each prisoner knows that the other has the same choice.

The real dilemma—the best strategy for each prisoner individually is to confess and blame the crime on the other. But it could provide a worse outcome.

Real-world application is about cooperating even when something isn't in your best interests.

The source of the information

Albert W. Tucker, book, *Contributions to the Theory of Games*, 1950

Developing critical thinking

1 Give students plenty of time to discuss their ideas in their groups, then hold a whole-class discussion giving guidance on examples if students struggle.

EXTENSION ACTIVITY

Write the following scenarios on the board. Ask students to discuss them in groups and to decide which gaming theory each one most reflects (1 = The Stag Hunt, 2 = the ultimatum).

1 During a governmental election, no one political party has enough votes to form a government. Party A has the most votes but can take power only if they can form a coalition with another party (Party B), but the two parties disagree on several important issues. If they can't form a coalition, then no party will have overall power. What should Party A and Party B do?

2 A house is for sale for $250,000. A married couple love the house but don't want to spend too much money. They think the house is worth $230,000. Should they offer $220,000, $230,000, or $250,000?

2 You may wish to mix up the groups to vary the task. Once students have discussed the questions, open this up for a whole-class discussion.

Language development: Prepositional verbs

Ask students to read the information in the *Prepositional verbs* box. Remind them that errors in the use of prepositions are very common amongst non-native speakers, so it is important for them to make a note of any verb + preposition collocations they come across.

1 Ask students to check their answers in pairs before feeding back to the whole class. To extend the task, ask students to write five of their own sentences using some of the prepositional verbs from this exercise.

ANSWERS			
1 with	3 for	5 on	7 to
2 to	4 in	6 for	8 for

2 Allow students plenty of time for this exercise, as they may initially find several places where they would like to insert an adverb, but there is only one way to complete the task successfully.

ANSWERS

1 glancing <u>quickly</u> through
2 refers <u>mainly</u> to
3 look <u>only</u> at
4 listen <u>carefully</u> to (Note that it's grammatically possible for *carefully* to come at the end of this sentence, too.)

Language development: Phrasal verbs

Draw students' attention to the information in the *Phrasal verbs* box. Highlight the fact that although phrasal verbs are not common in academic English, they are often used in spoken, informal English, so they are important in enhancing fluency.

1 Ask students to work in pairs to do the task before feeding back to the class.

ANSWERS	
1 prepositional verb	4 prepositional verb
2 phrasal verb	5 phrasal verb
3 phrasal verb	6 phrasal verb

2 Encourage students to attempt this exercise without a dictionary. They can then check their ideas by referring to a dictionary.

ANSWERS	
1 constitutes	4 examines
2 evaluates	5 fabricate
3 quit	6 discuss

3 Remind students that phrasal verbs are not generally used in academic contexts. Ask students to decide on the appropriate verbs. They can then compare their answers with a partner before feeding back to the whole class.

ANSWERS

1 stipulates—academic text (utilizes a formal single word rather than a phrasal verb)
2 ascertain—academic text (utilizes a formal single word rather than a phrasal verb)
3 BOTH—The sentence could be from a semi-formal magazine video game review. *Organizing* is more neutral.
4 support, increases—academic text (utilizes a formal single word rather than a phrasal verb)
5 BOTH—The sentence could be spoken in an informal/semi-formal context.
6 manage—academic text (utilizes a formal single word rather than a phrasal verb)
7 step up, take part—Reference to "she" suggests this is a spoken, informal context.

This is a good place to use the video resource *Reality TV: the harsh reality*. It is located in the Video resources section of the digital component.

EXTENSION ACTIVITY

Write the following sentences with phrasal verbs on the board and ask students to think of synonyms that would be more suitable for use in an academic text.

1 The research paper looked at the link between video games and learning abilities. (examined)
2 The electronic games industry was set up in the 1970s with the arrival of arcade games. (established)
3 The suggestion that gaming can increase violence in young people may put off parents from buying games for their children. (deter)
4 It is the responsibility of parents to set down restrictions on when and for how long their children can play video games. (impose)

SPEAKING Formulating a debate on banning violent electronic games

Pronunciation skill

Cultural awareness

The /r/ sound is often a problem area for language learners. Many European languages have a distinctive /r/ sound that is difficult for non-native speakers to replicate, e.g., Italians roll their /r/ sound, French speakers use their throat for their /r/ sound. In English, the /r/ sound is created at the front of the mouth, using the lips. East Asian students in particular tend to confuse the /r/ and /l/ sounds as they find it hard to activate the correct mouth muscles to create the /r/ sound. Try drilling a few words that use the /r/ sound, e.g., reality, creation, bravery, occurrence, retribution.

Ask students to read the *Identifying the linking* /r/ box. Read the example sentences aloud to demonstrate the /r/ sound occurring between the two vowel sounds.

1 Ask students to read the sentences and underline the linking /r/. Don't check their answers yet.
2 Play the audio and ask students to check their answers. During class feedback, invite individual students to practice pronouncing the sentences correctly.

AUDIO SCRIPT 1.09

1 I'm principally a lecturer at the university's Entertainment Technology Center.
2 He pinpoints video games as an area that gives us greater insight into how learning takes place.
3 No one can learn unless they are able to connect consequences to actions, especially when the consequences are in the distant future.
4 In real life there are, I read anyway, that there are few real zero-sum games.
5 There are two outcomes to the stag hunt. Either both hunters hunt the stag together, or both hunters hunt rabbits on their own.
6 Two drivers drive towards each other on a collision course.

ANSWERS

1 I'm principally a lecturer **at** the university's Entertainment Technology Center.
2 He pinpoints video games as an area that gives us greate**r in**sight into how learning takes place.
3 No one can learn unless they a**re a**ble to connect consequences to actions, especially when the consequences a**re in** the distant future.
4 In real life the**re ar**e, I read anyway, that the**re ar**e few real zero-sum games.
5 The**re ar**e two outcomes to the stag hunt. Either both hunters hunt the stag together, or both hunters hunt rabbits on thei**r own**.
6 Two drivers drive towards each othe**r on** a collision course.

Speaking skill

Cultural awareness

In some cultures, particularly East Asian cultures, it is considered rude to disagree with people, so bear in mind that some of your students may feel uncomfortable doing so. Encourage them to practice the skill of disagreeing, as it will be expected of them during seminar debates, but reassure them that by remaining polite they will not offend their fellow students in the process.

Refer students to the information in the *Agreeing and disagreeing—degrees of formality* box.

1 Ask students to read the statements in the chart, then play the audio. Students can then check their answers in pairs before feeding back to the class.

1

Student 1: That was an interesting lecture on video games today, wasn't it?

Student 2: Yeah, definitely.

Student 1: It makes sense to me that we can become better drivers by playing video games. I don't have my license yet, but I'm happy to know that I'm improving vital skills while playing video games.

Student 2: I'm with you on that one. However, I'm not so sure about gaming improving my creativity. You know the amount of time that I spend on different games, but I can't draw, and I've never written a decent story in my life!

Student 1: I'd say the exact opposite. The lecturer did provide strong evidence to suggest that it does, so I'll have to side with him on that one.

2

Student 1: So the Prisoner's Dilemma shows us that it's better to cooperate …

Student 2: I beg to differ. In this situation, the best outcome is to go free, which is only possible if you don't cooperate.

Student 1: I see your point, but I can't agree with you. If you don't cooperate, you risk five years in prison and you betray your partner.

Student 2: Yes, there's an element of risk—I would agree with that. But…

ANSWERS

Statement	Student 1	Student 2
We can become better drivers by playing video games.	✓	✓
Gaming can improve your creativity.	✓	✗
It's better to cooperate in the Prisoner's Dilemma situation.	✓	✗
The best outcome is only possible if you don't cooperate.	✗	✓

2   Ask this question to the whole class. If there is any confusion, play the audio again to clarify.

ANSWERS

The first dialogue is an informal conversation. A key marker for the informality is the line, "Yeah, definitely." The second dialogue has no markers of informality so is more likely to be a formal debate.

3   Remind students to use the phrases for agreeing and disagreeing during their discussions. Monitor and check that students are being polite when disagreeing. Make a note of any problem areas to follow up on.

SPEAKING TASK

Brainstorm and plan

Ask students to discuss the statement in the *Brainstorm* section in groups, then check their ideas with the whole class. They should understand that the statistics suggest a link between video games and an increase in aggressive behavior in boys.

Divide the class into three groups for the *Plan* section and ensure that each group understands what they need to do. Allow plenty of time for groups 1 and 2 to prepare their arguments, and for group 3 to plan their evaluation. Group 3 may wish to divide up items on the checklist to different students to make the evaluation stage easier.

Speak and share

Invite a member of group 3 to introduce the debate. Remind students to make notes when another group is speaking. During the discussion, monitor for language and also for the way that students present their arguments. After the discussion, allow time for students to read their notes to decide how they could counter argue.

For the *Share* section, group 3 should decide which group made the best argument and why. During this stage, monitor and take language notes. Use the photocopiable *Unit assignment checklist* on page 89 to assess the students' speaking.

Extra research task

Ask students to research the growth in female users of video games. Ask students to find out why this growth is occurring, and if there are any differences between male and female gamers. Advise students to look at gaming on social network sites such as Facebook as part of their research.

CRITICAL THINKING SKILLS Why develop critical thinking skills?

This page features material from Palgrave's *Critical Thinking Skills* by Stella Cottrell. The aim is to remind students of the importance of critical thinking skills and improved study skills practices generally. On this particular page, students are advised not to become complacent regarding their own critical thinking abilities. Remind students that being critical isn't about offering negative comments, but about questioning and analyzing information they are presented with. Critical thinking is an encouraged skill at college level. Ask students to read the information and to conduct an honest appraisal of their own skills. How can they be further improved? You could ask students to write up their appraisal in a reflective diary.

Nostalgia

Critical thinking	Organizing qualitative data Representative samples
Language development	Approximation Particularizer and exclusive adverbs
Pronunciation	Juncture
Speaking	Identifying sources of information

Discussion point

Direct students' attention to the picture on page 27. Ask them what they can see in the picture, what they think the picture might represent, and why the images are out of focus and faded. Encourage them to think about memories of the past and the feelings attached to those memories. The fact that the images are unclear and faded reflects the incomplete nature of our memories.

Refer students to the title of the unit: *Nostalgia*. Explain that it is a feeling meaning "a sentimental longing for the past." Do students think that it is positive or negative, or can it be either? Explain that it is more often associated with happy feelings, although it can also be connected with sad feelings.

Write on the board something that you would miss about your home and something you wouldn't (e.g., family, the high cost of living). Then allow students time to discuss the questions in pairs. The questions are hypothetical, but your students may actually be away from home, so adapt this task accordingly. After students have discussed the questions, ask for volunteers to share their answers with the class.

Vocabulary preview

1 Ask students to do the exercise without a dictionary. Have them work in pairs to explain the meanings to each other. During class feedback, make sure students can pronounce the words correctly. Pay particular attention to the word stress in the verb *recall* and the pronunciation of *reminisce*.

ANSWERS

1 remember	6 help (or make) you
2 have forgotten it	remember
3 having bad memories of	7 help (or make) you
4 forget about it	remember
5 brought back	8 remember (good times)

2 Ask students to work individually to organize the words. They can then check their answers with a partner before feeding back to the class.

ANSWERS

Remember: recall, get flashbacks, evoke, trigger, jog your memory, reminisce
Forget: slip your mind, put something behind you

3 Discuss this question as a class. Ask students how they decided which words are usually used in a negative context. They should mention the use of *terrible day* in the *flashbacks* sentence and the idea of moving on to thinking positively rather than negatively in the *put it behind you* sentence. Alert students to the fact that the term *flashbacks* is often used in connection with extremely traumatic events.

ANSWERS

get flashbacks, put something behind you

LISTENING 1 How to deal with homesickness

Before you listen

Ask students to work with a partner to rank the remedies, but stress that they need not agree. Discuss answers with the whole class.

EXTENSION ACTIVITY

Write the following sentences on the board:

1 It's best to disconnect from home for a while so that you can fully engage with your new environment.

2 It's best to keep connections with home through pictures, phone calls, and visits, as this will make the new environment easier to cope with.

Ask students to work in pairs to match the remedies to the two statements on the board. Are there any remedies that don't fit?

(Answers: 1 c, e, g; 2 a, b, f; d could be for either statement, depending on whether someone uses it to keep contact with old friends or to create links with new friends, h could also be for either.)

Ask students whether they think the majority of their class agrees with statement 1 or statement 2.

Listening

Write the following words on the board: *eagerness, apprehension, to drop out, sentimental, to embrace*. Ask students to identify the word family of each (e.g., noun, verb, adjective) and check that they can pronounce each correctly. To check students understand, write the following definitions on the board and ask students to match them to the words:

1 *showing intense interest* (eagerness, noun)
2 *to accept something willingly and happily* (to embrace, verb)
3 *to leave school or university before finishing a course* (to drop out, phrasal verb)
4 *showing fear of the future* (apprehension, noun)
5 *feelings of sadness or nostalgia; being emotional* (sentimental, adjective)

Tell the students they will hear these words in the audio.

1 Play the audio and ask students to do the exercise. Check the answers with the class.

AUDIO SCRIPT 1.11

Lecturer: Hello and welcome to our special podcast this week. As senior lecturer in psychology, I have been asked to organise a podcast dealing with homesickness among those students who have moved from faraway places to study for their degrees with us here in the south of England. Our own research survey shows that a little over 90% of first-year students at this university experience some level of homesickness. In due course we will hear from three of our second-year students who have agreed to share their experiences, but first of all let's consider what homesickness actually is. For many new students, the beginning of their university life generates both eagerness and apprehension. This could be about making the move, beginning academic work, or meeting new people. For some, this anxiety is quickly overcome as they adapt to their new environment; for others, the transition takes longer and sometimes develops into homesickness. The student longs for and becomes distressed over the loss of what is familiar and secure. Mostly it is the loss of people, but it can also include loss of routine, nostalgia for a place, or the simple knowledge that family life continues in a far-off place without them. In some of these cases, the student will be prone to the symptoms of homesickness several weeks before the move, for others, quite surprisingly, it may affect them much later—after the first holiday or even at the beginning of the second year. However, homesickness largely strikes within the first few days. Although homesickness is not a serious medical condition, it can result in distressing symptoms like sleeplessness, anxiety, and feeling tearful and emotional, and can lead to feelings of loneliness and isolation. Sometimes it means that an individual feels unable to fully engage with other people or take part in activities, both of which can be beneficial in the first few days or weeks of life away from home.

According to a report by the National Audit Office in the U.K., one in five students drop out after the first year of study. What was first known as Nostalgic Disease in sixteenth century Swiss literature is thought to be one of the most common causes of withdrawal from tertiary education courses each year.

Some of our students have taken part in a focus group on the topic of homesickness, and they've very kindly agreed to let me share extracts from the recording.

First of all we asked each student to introduce themselves and tell us how homesickness had affected them. Here's what they said …

Nicola: Hi, I'm Nicola from California. When I came last year it was the first time I'd ever been to the U.K. And I … um … really felt like an outsider here in the beginning. The lifestyle, the people, and the weather were all very different from what I was used to. I sort of felt anxious and insecure … and I found it really difficult to concentrate on anything. I was really forgetful— everything just seemed to slip my mind, and my work suffered a lot in the first few months.

Amanda: Hello, I'm Amanda from the north of England. It was the first time I'd been away from home, and I felt really lost. My homesickness actually gave me physical symptoms. I really had difficulty eating and sleeping, and I ended up being quite ill for most of the first term. You know: severe headaches, feeling dizzy—that type of thing. As a result, I missed a lot of lectures, and I scored really low marks on all of my assignments in the first term. I had joined a few different clubs in the first week, but eventually I stopped going to them, too.

Chloe: Hey, there. I'm Chloe from Australia. My first year was awful—university sort of felt like a prison. I didn't know anyone at all, and there was nothing to do but study. Maybe that was my own fault. I suppose I could have made more of an effort to meet people. But, in the end I locked myself away in my room and hardly saw anyone. Before long I was suffering from depression. I lost confidence in my own ability and ended up losing interest in the course. I stopped doing research for assignments and ended up failing the first year exams.

Lecturer: As I said before, homesickness is not a serious medical condition. However, depression and anxiety are, and for these help should be sought from your doctor. For mild cases of homesickness, counselling can be extremely beneficial. The next question we asked the students in our focus group was: what did you do to help you get over homesickness? And, what advice would you give to those students suffering from homesickness at the moment? Here's what they said.

First, Nicola …

Nicola: Well, I guess that calling home was what made me really settle down. You have to understand that your family and friends are only a phone call away. Just hearing my parents' voices on the other end of the line always calmed me down. I even used webcam chats—they really made up for the lack of face-to-face contact. It's not totally the same, but it was a big help. I didn't overdo it—I mean, I didn't call home every day. I only called when something new happened, you know, when I bought something or met new people. Using social networks is also a great way to catch up with your friends, and it makes you feel like you're still with them back home. Just sharing jokes, photos, and experiences every day brings them closer to you.

Lecturer: Then, this is what Amanda had to say …

Amanda: I had way too much contact with my family during my first term. I realised that going home every weekend was actually making me feel worse. What

I would advise is to get out there and make contact with the people around you. You're not the only one who's going through this because your classmates are in the same boat as you. Talk to them and ask them how they're dealing with things. This gives you a great opportunity to make new mates. It also allows you to form your own support network, meaning you can get over common difficulties together. Listening to other people's problems can also put yours into perspective. Meeting new people helps put homesickness out of your mind and allows you to embrace your new environment. I joined a film club, which helped me meet more people.

Lecturer: And here are Chloe's thoughts on the subject …

Chloe: You really have to put those negative thoughts behind you—that's what I did. I found that a good way to get rid of that homesick feeling was to always have something that has sentimental value with me. When I was younger, it would be a teddy bear or a blanket, but as I got older I discovered that I still needed my comfort objects. By that I mean photos, my own pillow, a familiar perfume or cologne, favourite music, films, or even an old diary. Having familiar things around you can help you feel more at ease. In fact, I looked at photos from when I was in Australia, and even set up my new room like my old one was. It really helped jog my memory on how happy I always felt in my bedroom when I was younger.

ANSWERS
Nicola: d and f   **Amanda:** c and e   **Chloe:** a and b

---

2   Draw students' attention to the *Academic keywords* box. Check that students can pronounce these words correctly and that they are clear on the meanings. Then refer students to the table. Play the audio and ask them to complete the table. They can then check their answers in pairs before feeding back to the class.

AUDIO SCRIPT   1.12

Nicola: Hi, I'm Nicola from California. When I came last year it was the first time I'd ever been to the U.K. And I … um … really felt like an outsider here in the beginning. The lifestyle, the people, and the weather were all very different from what I was used to. I sort of felt anxious and insecure … and I found it really difficult to concentrate on anything. I was really forgetful—everything just seemed to slip my mind, and my work suffered a lot in the first few months.

Amanda: Hello, I'm Amanda from the north of England. It was the first time I'd been away from home, and I felt really lost. My homesickness actually gave me physical symptoms. I really had difficulty eating and sleeping, and I ended up being quite ill for most of the first term. You know: severe headaches, feeling dizzy—that type of thing. As a result, I missed a lot of lectures, and I scored really low marks on all of my assignments in the first term. I had joined a few different clubs in the first week, but eventually I stopped going to them, too.

Chloe: Hey, there. I'm Chloe from Australia. My first year was awful—university sort of felt like a prison. I didn't know anyone at all, and there was nothing to do but study. Maybe that was my own fault. I suppose I could have made more of an effort to meet people. But, in the end I locked myself away in my room and hardly saw anyone. Before long I was suffering from depression. I lost confidence in my own ability and ended up losing interest in the course. I stopped doing research for assignments and ended up failing the first year exams.

ANSWERS

Student	Feel when first arrived?	Feel afterwards?
Nicola	Felt like an outsider, anxious and insecure. Was forgetful in terms of course work.	Settled and calm.
Amanda	Had difficulty eating and sleeping. Felt ill—dizzy and had headaches.	Ready to embrace her new environment.
Chloe	Felt depressed and disinterested. Lacked confidence.	Felt more at ease.

Critical thinking skill

Refer students to the *Organizing qualitative data* box and ask them to read it carefully. Ask them what methods they might use to gather qualitative data (e.g., interviews, focus groups, observations).

EXTENSION ACTIVITY

Ask students to work in groups to list the advantages and disadvantages of qualitative and quantitative research. Possible points:

Quantitative

Advantages: easier to measure and analyze; more objective as researcher is less involved with participants

Disadvantages: need a large sample to make meaningful conclusions; don't get in-depth findings

Qualitative

Advantages: get rich, in-depth data about people's experiences

Disadvantages: findings cannot be applied to wider population; data more difficult to analyze

---

1   Ask students to read the raw data and cross out the two incorrect items. Check their answers as a class.

ANSWERS

different lifestyle, people, & weather and *language barriers* are causes of homesickness rather than effects.

---

2 Students complete the table in pairs. Check the answers with the class.

ANSWERS			
1 Suffered physical symptoms	2 Suffered psychological symptoms	3 Studies were affected	4 Social life was affected
loss of appetite headaches & dizziness	felt anxious & insecure sleeping problems difficulty concentrating forgetfulness depression	missed lectures scored low grades lost interest in course neglected research assignment failed exams	stopped going to clubs lost confidence

3 Play the extract and ask students to write the numbers next to the names.

ANSWERS
Nicola: 2, 3   **Amanda:** 1   **Chloe:** 2, 3, 4

Developing critical thinking

Refer students back to page 28 and their ideas about effective remedies. Ask groups to discuss the three questions. Allow plenty of time for group discussion, then ask groups to share their ideas with the class.

Cultural awareness

Question 3 in this section allows for discussion of how people deal with problems differently. In some cultures, there is a lot of stigma attached to psychological problems and people do not talk about issues openly. Be aware that your students may believe it is preferable to keep problems to yourself.

LISTENING 2 Memory and smell

Before you listen

1 Ask students to add more smells to the list and then rank them individually.

2 Ask students to compare their lists with a partner.

Listening

Refer students to the *Academic keywords* box. Ensure they are clear on meanings and pronunciation, and encourage them to write the words in their notebooks.

Ask students to look at the information in the mind map. Then play the audio and have them take notes on the mind map as they listen. Ask students to compare their answers with a partner.

AUDIO SCRIPT   1.13
Professor: Good morning, everyone. Let's move on from our initial studies of nostalgia by recapping what we discovered in our previous lesson. Well, we've now seen that nostalgia can be described as a yearning to return to our past. We can also say that rather than reminiscing about our real past, we tend to conjure up a romanticised version of it—psychoanalysis calls this screen memory because we're inclined to filter out the negative experiences to give us an ideal version of what really happened. Remember that we came to the conclusion that nostalgia did not refer to any specific memories; a more accurate description would be that of an emotional state.

Now, this morning we're going to look at more research in this area that suggests that these past emotions are particularly connected to the sounds, smells, and images that we experienced simultaneously with those feelings. I should add that all the senses may be used to trigger the nostalgic experience: hearing music, touching a fabric, tasting a particular food, seeing photographs, but one of the most powerful is smell. This is sometimes known as olfactory-evoked recall.

Nearly everyone has experienced a moment when a smell has made them recall a long-lost memory from the distant past. It may be the smell of chlorine reminding you of a summer spent splashing around in a swimming pool, the perfume of a long-lost friend, or the aroma of freshly baked bread taking you back to your grandmother's kitchen. The smell of wood smoke can put a nostalgic smile on our faces as we look back on a summer camping trip from our childhood, whereas the smell of mouthwash may give us a flashback to a rather unpleasant trip to the dentist.

Why do smells produce such strong emotions? How can a smell bring back memories and call up powerful responses almost instantaneously? The reason is the olfactory bulb, which is a part of the brain responsible for the perception of odours, is also part of the brain's limbic system, an area so closely linked with memory and feeling that it's sometimes called the "emotional brain." Research has shown that when areas of the brain connected to memory are damaged, the ability to identify smells is actually impaired.

Let's consider how powerful olfactory-evoked recall can actually be. I would like to refer to Dr. Johan Willander's study of groups of adults, whose average age was 75; the researchers offered three different sets of the same 20 memory prompts—the prompt as a word, the prompt as a picture, and the prompt as a smell. The scientists found that the word and visual cues brought back memories mainly from subjects' adolescence and young adulthood. However, the smell prompts called up recollections from early childhood, under the age of ten. Despite such memories coming from the extremely distant past, the volunteers claimed that they tended to convey the sudden sensation of being taken back in time—they described these memories much more clearly.

The ability of smells to trigger autobiographical memories that are exceedingly graphic and detailed is widely known as the Proust phenomenon. According to

Marcel Proust in his novel *In Search of Lost Time,* odour and taste trigger very emotional and detailed memory recall. However, Proust's ideas were expressed in a novel. Is there any scientific research to support the idea that olfactory stimuli can provoke long-term memories more effectively than other sensory stimuli? And how do we determine the concept that olfactory-evoked recall methods are useful to us in possible treatment of patients?

If we can find evidence, then we should be able to apply this knowledge to our particular area of interest this week, which is the treatment of post-traumatic stress disorder or PTSD. As we've discussed before, PTSD is an anxiety disorder that can develop after experiencing any event that is psychologically traumatic.

Let's refer to the study by Toffolo *et al* at Utrecht University from 2011. In an experiment aimed at investigating aversive memories, similar to those experienced by PTSD patients, 70 healthy women watched a film designed to provoke aversion—the scenes in the film included a car accident, genocide, and a circus accident involving people being trod on by an elephant. They were also simultaneously exposed to <u>olfactory, auditory, and visual</u> triggers—a particular smell, coloured lights on a black wall, and neutral background music. One week later the participants were exposed to only one of the three stimulants and asked to relate their memories of the film. The results revealed that smell-evoked memories of aversive events were more detailed than those evoked by auditory triggers. Visual triggers were also more effective than auditory ones.

The findings of that study concluded that smells are more effective than music when triggering traumatic memories and are as effective as visual stimuli. Remember that music has always been considered to provide equally powerful memory triggers. We should also note that because all of the participants were women, the research does not include the whole human population. Nevertheless, research by Tolin and Foa proves that more women than men suffer from PTSD—therefore the results are meaningful for this particular group. So, how can olfactory-evoked recall methods be useful in the treatment of PTSD patients? Let us now look at a real case study. Can you all turn to page …

POSSIBLE ANSWERS
- Examples of smells and memories: *the smell of chlorine—a summer spent splashing around in a swimming pool*
  perfume—a long-lost friend
  freshly baked bread—your grandmother's kitchen
  wood smoke—a summer camping trip
  mouthwash—an unpleasant trip to the dentist
- Why do smells produce strong emotions?
  The same part of the brain is responsible for memory, feeling, and smell.

- Johan Willander's research: *Smell prompts brought back the most vivid and earliest (early childhood) memories.*
- Toffolo's experiment: *Smell and visual prompts brought back stronger memories of aversive events.*

Critical thinking skill

Ask the students to read the information in the *Representative samples* box. Remind them that in order for research to have true validity, the sample it uses must be representative. They need to ensure that they bear this in mind with their own academic research.

1 Play the audio and ask students to make notes in the table. *repeated extracts*

AUDIO SCRIPT 1.14
Professor: Let's consider how powerful olfactory-evoked recall can actually be. I would like to refer to Dr. Johan Willander's study of groups of adults, whose average age was 75; the researchers offered three different sets of the same 20 memory prompts—the prompt as a word, the prompt as a picture, and the prompt as a smell. The scientists found that the word and visual cues brought back memories mainly from subjects' adolescence and young adulthood. However, the smell prompts called up recollections from early childhood, under the age of ten. Despite such memories coming from the extremely distant past, the volunteers claimed that they tended to convey the sudden sensation of being taken back in time—they described these memories much more clearly. *(fades)*

The ability of smells to trigger autobiographical memories … experiencing any event that is psychologically traumatic.

Let's refer to the study by Toffolo *et al* at Utrecht University from 2011. In an experiment aimed at investigating aversive memories, similar to those experienced by PTSD patients, 70 healthy women watched a film designed to provoke aversion—the scenes in the film included a car accident, genocide, and a circus accident involving people being trod on by an elephant. They were also simultaneously exposed to olfactory, auditory, and visual triggers—a particular smell, coloured lights on a black wall, and neutral background music. One week later the participants were exposed to only one of the three stimulants and asked to relate their memories of the film. The results revealed that smell-evoked memories of aversive events were more detailed than those evoked by auditory triggers. Visual triggers were also more effective than auditory ones.

The findings of that study concluded that smells are more effective than music when triggering traumatic memories, and are as effective as visual stimuli. Remember that music has always been considered to provide equally powerful memory triggers. We should also note that because all of the participants were women, the research does not include the whole human population. Nevertheless, research by Tolin and Foa proves that more women than men suffer from PTSD—therefore the results are meaningful for this particular group. So, how can olfactory-evoked recall methods be useful in the treatment of PTSD patients? Let us now look at a real case study. Can you all turn to page …

ANSWERS
Willander
1 no
2 Average age was 75
3 Participants' childhood was a long time ago—better test of how powerful the memory prompts are
Toffolo *et al*
1 no
2 All female, all healthy
3 More women than men suffer from PTSD

2 Have students work in pairs to make a list of characteristics to make a representative sample and then ask each pair to feed back to the class. Encourage the students to comment on each other's lists.

Developing critical thinking

1 Describe a smell connected to a good memory for you and one connected to a bad memory. Invite students to ask you more questions about these smells. They can then discuss the questions in a group.

2 Ask the students to discuss the questions in groups. Then have a whole-class feedback session.

Language development: Approximation

Ask students to read the information in the *Approximation* box. Remind them that approximation language can also be used to convey the writer's attitude, as demonstrated in the final two examples.

1 Ask students to work individually to complete the phrases, then check their answers in pairs.

ANSWERS
1 round <u>about</u>
2 a little <u>over</u>
3 up <u>to</u>
4 something <u>like</u>
5 or <u>so</u>
6 just short <u>of</u>

2 Ask students to work with a partner to organize the phrases in exercise 1 into categories.

ANSWERS
Approximately: round about; something like; or so
Less than, but including: up to; just short of
More: a little over

3 Ask students to do this exercise individually. Check answers as a class.

ANSWERS
1 **Up to** 50 students per course.
2 **under / nearly / almost / around / round about** 10 seconds
3 **(just) over / upwards of / somewhere in the region of / something like** 100 scientific papers
4 I completed the test in **less than / under** 30 minutes.
5 Zara scored **nearly / almost** 90% on the test. She's very smart!
6 The university is relatively new; it was built **less than / under** 20 years ago.

Language development: Particulizer and exclusive adverbs

Ask students to read the information in the *Particulizer and exclusive adverbs* box, then do the exercise. Ask students what helped them decide on their answers.

ANSWERS
1 particularly   4 especially
2 solely   5 Mostly
3 precisely   6 Only

SPEAKING Conducting a survey on memory

Pronunciation skill

Refer students to the information in the *Juncture* box and remind them how important juncture is if they want to improve their spoken fluency in English. Have them mark the places where there is juncture in the sentences. While they are doing so, write them on the board to refer to after listening. Play the audio, then check the answers with the class. Invite individual students to come to the board to mark the junctures in each sentence.

AUDIO SCRIPT   1.15
1 The student longs for and becomes distressed over the loss of what is familiar and secure.
2 According to the Office of National Statistics, one in five students drop out after the first year of study.
3 When I came last year it was the first time I'd ever been to the U.K.
4 What I would advise is to get out there and make contact with the people around you.
5 In fact, I looked at photos from when I was in Australia.
6 In an experiment aiming to investigate aversive memories, similar to those experienced by PTSD patients …

ANSWERS

1 The student longs fo**r a**nd becomes distresse**d o**ver the **l**oss **of** wha**t is** familia**r a**nd secure.

2 According to the Office of National Statistics, o**ne i**n five students dro**p ou**t after the first yea**r of** study.

3 Whe**n I** came last yea**r it** was the first ti**me I'd e**ver been to the U.K.

4 Wha**t I** would **a**dvi**se is** t**o ge**t ou**t** the**re a**nd make contact with the peop**le a**round you.

5 In fact, I looke**d at** photos from whe**n I** wa**s i**n Au**s**tralia.

6 I**n an e**xperimen**t ai**ming to investiga**te a**versive memories, similar **to tho**se **e**xperienced by PTSD patients …

This is a good place to use the video resource *Retro-volution*. It is located in the Video resources section of the digital component.

Speaking skill

Ask students to read the *Identifying sources of information* box. Remind them that authentic sources are not only important in their written academic work, but also in academic contexts where they are expected to speak (e.g., seminars and presentations). Students can assess the extracts in pairs before sharing their ideas with the class.

POSSIBLE ANSWERS

a O (newspaper)

b S (magazine)

c S (academic journal)

d P (results from an experiment)

e O (radio talk show)

SPEAKING TASK

Brainstorm

Ask students to work in pairs to choose their topic. Encourage them to make notes during their brainstorm.

Plan

1 Ask students to read the example. Explain that it is connected to the topic of childhood memories. Pairs should now list the objectives for their chosen topic, and decide on the questions they will need to ask to find the answers and what type of questions those will be.

2 Have students decide how many people to interview. If you have a limited amount of time, restrict their surveys to the classroom. However, if you have more time, you could ask students to widen their research to people outside of their class as part of their homework.

Speak and share

When the interviews are finished, pairs should come back together to discuss their findings and to prepare a presentation for another pair. Encourage them to use the approximation language from page 32.

If you prefer, have students prepare the presentations for homework so that they can present them in the next class. Encourage students to evaluate the other presentations and to ask questions. During this stage, monitor and take language notes. Use the photocopiable *Unit assignment checklist* on page 90 to assess the students' speaking.

Extra research task

Ask students to research their chosen topic from this speaking task online. This will enable them to include secondary sources in their research. They should be prepared to share their online research in the next class and to discuss whether it supports the findings from their interviews or not, and if not, why not.

STUDY SKILLS Listening to extended lectures

Getting started

After pairs have discussed the questions, open this up to the class. Remind students that listening to authentic news reports on the radio, TV, or online is good practice and will expose them to a variety of native speaker accents at high speeds.

Scenario

Ask students to read and make a note of what Imran could do to overcome his problems.

POSSIBLE ANSWER

Imran needs more listening practice. As he finds accents problematic, he could listen to local media and watch the TV news for that region each day. He could also join some social clubs with other local students. Imran should focus on taking notes of only the key words and key points. He could form or join a study group to help consolidate his ideas about things he thought he had heard, or wasn't sure about. He could also practice taking notes from online presentations which feature a multi-media mix.

Consider it

Ask students to discuss these tips with a partner before opening the discussion up to the whole class.

Over to you

After pairs have discussed the questions, have a whole-class discussion and write any other tips or techniques on the board.

Critical thinking	Using illustrative examples to support an argument Anticipating a conclusion based on reasons and evidence
Language development	Nominalization Possible, probable, and hypothetical future predictions
Pronunciation	Word stress in word families
Speaking	Managing conversation

Discussion point

Direct students' attention to the picture on page 37. Ask them what is happening in the picture and what risks the people are taking (a stunt where two people are attempting to fly with a makeshift plane and are risking injury or possible death if they fall).

Then ask students to work in pairs to discuss the questions. To help start them off you could describe someone you know who takes risks.

Cultural awareness

Bear in mind that a discussion of risk-taking behavior may encompass some sensitive topics, such as drinking, gambling, promiscuity, and drugs. These topics are taboo in many cultures, so you may need to steer the discussion to less controversial activities, such as fast or reckless driving, extreme sports, cigarette smoking, risky financial investments, etc.

Vocabulary preview

Write the word *risk* on the board. Ask students what class of word it is (a noun and a verb). Brainstorm any collocations that students already know for both the noun and the verb. Remind them that when learning vocabulary they should always pay attention to common collocations, as knowledge of these language chunks will allow them to become more fluent in both their spoken and written language.

1 Ask students to choose the correct words in the sentences. They can then check their answers in pairs before feeding back to the class.

ANSWERS
1	fatalities	6	unregulated
2	run	7	faced
3	take	8	say
4	poses	9	odds
5	steel	10	on-the-job

2 Remind students they only need to choose three expressions. When they have written their sentences, ask them to check the sentences in pairs. Assist with any required correction. Invite volunteers to write some examples on the board.

3 Students can check their answers in pairs before whole-class feedback. Draw their attention to the use of the word *of* where *risk* is used as a noun in sentences 1 and 2, and to the verb form in 3.

ANSWERS
1 Smokers have a high risk of getting cancer.
2 If you eat too much, you run the risk of having health problems.
3 If you don't lock up your bicycle, you risk losing it.
Rule:
Risk (verb) is followed by the *-ing* form of the verb, not the infinitive.
Risk (noun) is followed by the preposition *of* and the *-ing* form of the verb.

LISTENING 1 The world's most dangerous jobs

Before you listen

Allow plenty of time for pairs to list and rank the jobs. Then invite students to share their ideas with the class.

Listening

1 Write the nine jobs from the box on the board. Have a class discussion and try to agree on a ranking for these jobs (1 = most dangerous). Then ask students how many of the jobs would make it onto the list of the world's most dangerous.

2 Before playing the audio, ask students to look at the *Academic keywords* box. Check that they can pronounce the words correctly and ensure they are clear on meanings. Encourage them to make a note of the words. Play the audio, then ask students to compare their ideas on the board with what they heard.

AUDIO SCRIPT 1.16
Presenter: Good afternoon and welcome back to World of Work. In this week's podcast we look at the most dangerous jobs in the world. Now, we all know that many jobs come with health risks. If you sit in front of a computer or in an office all day, you run the risk of getting stress, eye strain, and back problems. But some jobs are much more dangerous and can in fact

kill you. Crashing into a fiery explosion, being crushed by heavy equipment, or falling from a great height are on-the-job dangers that many workers face every single day. Joining us in the studio is Dr. Michael White, an expert on risky jobs, from California. Based on his own research and figures worldwide, he has recently drawn up a list of the most dangerous jobs in the world, and he is going to share some of them with us today. Welcome, Michael.

Michael: Thank you for having me.

Presenter: So, let's get started. The first job you have on your list is, quite frankly, one I had never even considered. Fisherman?

Michael: That's right, Peter. Being a fisherman is an extremely dangerous job. According to the United Nations Fisheries and Aquaculture Department, it's probably the most dangerous job in the world. Data collected from countries show that occupational fatalities in fishing industries far exceed the national average. For example, in Australia the fatality rate for fishers is 143 per 100,000 compared with 8.1 per 100,000 nationally. In the USA, the fatality rates for fishers is 25 to 30 times the national average. These figures are not only high, but they are not going down either. In fact, according to the United Nations Fisheries Department, they may be rising.

Presenter: Why is it so dangerous? Why so many fatalities?

Michael: The danger comes from hauling nets or cages that weigh hundreds of pounds. This in itself poses great risks, but now imagine the same with ice cold waves, wind, and heavy rain hitting you from all sides.

Presenter: Not to mention the risk of drowning, I suppose?

Michael: Yes, exactly.

Presenter: So fishing can be considered a very dangerous pursuit indeed. What next?

Michael: Well, although this does not rank quite as high in the U.S., it's certainly a very high-risk job in many other countries. Window cleaners.

Presenter: Window cleaners?

Michael: Yes. Especially the people who clean the outside of windows on tall skyscrapers. Frankly, you would need nerves of steel to do this job. High winds and surfaces slippery with soapy water can, of course, cause you to fall, which is the main cause of death in this profession. That being said, it's very hard to get statistics worldwide on window cleaning, as in many countries it's an unregulated profession.

Presenter: Every time I see someone cleaning one of those very tall buildings on the outside it always makes me nervous.

Michael: Yes, me too. But curiously, the majority of accidents with window cleaners come from falling off a ladder while cleaning windows that are not so high off the ground. The misuse of ladders is one of the leading causes of fall-related injuries and deaths according to the International Window Cleaning Association.

Presenter: Really?

Michael: Yes, and this number could be reduced by offering safety training to people responsible for setting up window cleaning equipment. The issue of safety training is one that comes up again and again in many dangerous professions, like window cleaning or construction. Window cleaners suffer many of the same risks as those working on construction sites. Construction work is also very dangerous for falls and accidents.

Presenter: I can imagine so.

Michael: The next job on the list is also one that many people don't consider automatically as a dangerous one. It's loggers.

Presenter: Loggers. People who cut down trees? Why is that so dangerous?

Michael: Well, loggers work on unstable, uneven terrain, such as mountain slopes. They are also working at great heights, with chain saws and logging machines that are dangerous even when used properly. Add to that the need to watch out for the momentum and massive weight of a huge falling branch or an entire tree. This work has to take place in all kinds of weather, and if a tree is not cut down properly, it can come crashing down in a completely different direction and roll violently down a slope, crushing anyone in its path.

Now, statistics for logging fatalities are not as high as those of fisheries or construction, but it can still be classified as a high-risk occupation and regularly makes the lists of "dangerous occupations" by bodies such as the United States Labor Bureau.

Presenter: Well. Here I was thinking you would be talking about bodyguards, stuntmen, spies, or other jobs like that. Instead we're discussing fishing, logging, construction, and window cleaning.

Michael: Don't get me wrong. It's safe to say that those other jobs you mention also entail risks. But there are, in fact, far fewer accidents in those areas than in the more mundane professions I've been outlining. There is considerably less glamor, and lots more danger.

Presenter: Thank you very much for joining us today.

Michael: My pleasure.

ANSWERS
construction worker, logger, fisherman, window cleaner

Critical thinking skill

Refer students to the *Using illustrative examples to support an argument* box and ask them to read it carefully. Remind students that the examples include extremely descriptive vocabulary, e.g., *being crushed by heavy equipment* rather than just *heavy equipment falls on you*. This use of vocabulary is far more engaging and makes it easier to persuade your audience to agree with an argument.

Ask students to write the jobs as they listen to the audio again. They can check their answers in pairs and come up with other examples for each job together. Remind students to use illustrative examples. Invite students to share their answers and additional examples with the class.

ANSWERS

1 window cleaner	6 logger
2 fisherman	7 fisherman / window cleaner
3 logger	
4 logger	8 logger
5 fisherman	

EXTENSION ACTIVITY

Ask students to brainstorm any other dangerous jobs that were not mentioned, e.g., oil rig worker, people in the military, firefighter, police officer, nuclear engineer.

Ask them to work in groups and discuss the risks attached to the jobs they have listed. Encourage them to use illustrative language. Then ask groups to discuss this question: What would encourage a person to do each of these dangerous jobs?

During class feedback, find out if students mentioned the following: money, physical challenge, the need to make a difference, prestige/status, power. Ask if they would be attracted to any of these jobs and why.

Developing critical thinking

Allow plenty of time for groups to discuss the questions. Note that question 4 may be a sensitive area if you are teaching a multinational group, so you may wish to steer the discussion to non-offensive topics, such as attitudes to motorbike helmets, seat belts, rates of smoking, etc.

This is a good place to use the video resource *Risky business*. It is located in the Video resources section of the digital component.

LISTENING 2 What is acceptable risk?

Before you listen

1 Ask students to first complete the questionnaire individually. They can then compare their answers in pairs and decide who is more of a risk-taker.

2 Ask pairs to write a definition together. Invite pairs to share their definitions and write a few on the board. Don't comment at this point, but tell students they will hear more about this term in the audio.

POSSIBLE ANSWER

Acceptable risk means a level of risk people are willing to take.

Listening

1 Play the audio. Discuss the definition of "acceptable risk" with the class. Compare it with the definitions they came up with. Then check that students understood the professor's purpose in the seminar.

Why the fake U.S. accents?
Why all female seminar?

AUDIO SCRIPT 1.17

Professor: Welcome back, everyone. I'd like us to take a break from looking at environmental law to discuss safety and danger in more general terms. You've all been given some reading about risk to do. I'd like to start by asking you all a question. Is it possible to ever really be completely safe from danger?

Class: Yes. / No. / Not sure.

Professor: We can all think of examples of activities that we think are safe, but we can also imagine that for each safe activity there is a possibility of danger.

Student 1: Can we say an activity is safe if the possibility of danger is very, very small?

Professor: Hmm. Perhaps. But let's take two activities. Climbing a mountain and driving a car. Both are dangerous activities. And in fact, more people die from car accidents than mountain accidents. In the United States, according to the Alpine Club of America, there are 25 deaths on average per year from mountain climbing. But there are between 30 and 40 thousand deaths from car accidents every year as well, according to the U.S. Census. So why do most people feel that driving a car is safer?

Student 1: It's easier than climbing a mountain.

Student 2: Maybe it's because it's a danger we can control. So it feels safer.

Professor: But it's still not without risks. One of the first points we have to understand is that safety is NOT the same as zero risk. So what makes us willing to engage in an activity that has risk? Or, more to the point, why would most people, given the choice, prefer to take the risk of getting in a car as opposed to hanging off the side of the mountain? The answer lies in the notion of acceptable risk. Does anyone have a definition of this?

Student 1: Yes, I've got it here. "Acceptable risk" describes an unwanted event which can meet any one of these categories: 1. it's very unlikely to happen; 2. the consequences of the event are not very serious; 3. the benefits of taking the risk are great.

Professor: Very good. We have the concept of acceptable risk because we know that absolute safety is almost impossible to achieve.

Student 2: Acceptable risk is often discussed in decisions about environmental health and safety, right?

Professor: Exactly. Does anyone else have anything on that? … For example, is there a measurement of acceptable risk?

Student 1: I read that many authorities are reluctant to specify what is an acceptable risk. Which, I guess, is understandable …

Student 2: If the chance of something bad happening is really, really small …

Student 1: But how small is really small?

Professor: Well, there is one measurement that has emerged. The one-in-a-million measurement. Have any of you come across that? It originated in the 1960s in the United States and is now widely used around the world, including by the World Health Organization. Let's say you are responsible for deciding if a certain product, like a shampoo or a kind of medicine, is dangerous. The one-in-a-million test asks, "Does this substance (shampoo, or medicine) have more than a one-in-a-million chance of causing death?"

Student 1: One in a million feels pretty safe.

Professor: Yes, it does. But it's not 100% safe. Let's look at another example. Clean drinking water in a city. How do you decide if it is dangerous or safe? And if it's safe, what is a safe level? Well, if the local health administration decided that by drinking the local water over a lifetime the chances of a person dying from drinking that water were one in a million or less, then that would be considered acceptable risk.

Student 2: Makes sense. I guess the same concept can be used for all kinds of things?

Professor: Of course. Acceptable risk informs decisions about what we drink, about the food we eat, about the products that are sold to us, and about the activities we are allowed by law to do.

Student 1: But professor, you mentioned at the beginning something about driving cars? The risk of having a fatal car accident is more than one in a million. I've got it here, at least in the figures for the U.K. The odds of dying in a car accident in the U.K. are 1 in 240.

Student 2: And probably more in this city.

Professor: Very good point. Over a lifetime of driving, the risk to your life is much more than one in a million. In some places, it's a lot more than the figure of 1 in 240 that was just quoted. And we still allow it, and everyone does it. Remember we had three aspects to the definition of acceptable risk? The first was that the event was unlikely to happen, the second was that the consequences of the event were small, and the third was …

Student 2: That the benefits of taking the risk were great.

Professor: Yes. A higher level of acceptable risk may in fact be tolerated if the benefits are considered much larger. Additionally, we may also tolerate higher risks if they are voluntary—if we choose to take them—than if they are involuntary. Feeling in control will help us tolerate higher risk.

Student 1: And I guess people have a sense of control when they drive. I mean, people feel more in control driving a car than taking an airplane, I guess. And I know that airplane accidents are a lot less common than car accidents, which means technically it's safer. But I feel that it's riskier …

Professor: Indeed. So. To conclude …

ANSWERS

The student in the audio says that acceptable risk describes an unwanted event that can meet any one of three categories.

The professor's purpose is to explain the concept of acceptable risk.

2 Before you play the audio again, allow students to try the exercise using what they can remember. Then play the audio so that students can complete their answers. Check the answers as a class, then refer students to the *Academic keywords* box. Drill the words to assess students' pronunciation. Encourage the use of the schwa sound in the first syllable of *acceptable*.

ANSWERS

1 F 2 T 3 T 4 T 5 F 6 T 7 NG 8 T

EXTENSION ACTIVITY

Write the following questions on the board and ask students to discuss them in pairs or small groups.

1 What risks have you taken so far today?

2 Which of the following do you think are acceptable risks and why?

- eating out-of-date meat
- driving over the speed limit on the motorway
- investing all your savings in a new company
- leaving your house unlocked all day
- smoking 20 cigarettes a day despite the known health effects

Monitor and circulate, noting any language issues and any interesting points that students make. Open the discussion up to the class and give any necessary language feedback.

Critical thinking skill

Ask students to read the information in the *Anticipating a conclusion based on reasons and evidence* box. Highlight that anticipating a conclusion is useful as it demonstrates how well you have understood a talk.

1 When students have chosen a conclusion, they can compare their answers with a partner. Encourage them to give reasons for their choice.

2 Play the audio, then check the answer with the class.

AUDIO SCRIPT   1.18

Professor: In the end, we still come back to the notion that danger exists everywhere. There is nothing in life that is completely risk-free. We just have to learn how to manage it, and live with it.

ANSWER
2

3 Ask students to listen to the lecture again and check the relevant sentences.

ANSWER
Checked sentences should be: 1, 3, 5, 7

Developing critical thinking

1 Circulate and monitor as the groups discuss the questions. Make a note of any language errors for correction. Also make a note of interesting points that are raised and encourage groups to share ideas with the class.

2 Ask students to discuss the questions in groups.

Language development: Nominalization

Refer students to the *Nominalization* box and ask them to read it carefully. Highlight the fact that nouns and noun phrases are far more common in academic English than verb phrases, so it is really important for them to develop this aspect of their vocabulary. Check that they know what suffixes are (endings to words).

1 Students should work individually. They can then check their answers in pairs before feeding back to the class.

ANSWERS

active (adj)	explode (verb)
dangerous (adj)	measure (verb)
disappoint (verb)	organize (verb)
drown (verb)	safe (adj)

2 When the students have finished, write the answers on the board to ensure students are clear on spelling, particularly when suffixes alter the spelling slightly (e.g., *generous—generosity*).

ANSWERS

achievement	generosity
decision	insecurity
expansion	involvement
expectation	uncertainty

3 Students can refer to their dictionaries for help if necessary. Have them compare their answers with a partner before feeding back to the whole class.

POSSIBLE ANSWERS
1 The company has made an investment of millions of dollars in risk assessment.
2 The government questions the accuracy of this report.
3 Do not underestimate the seriousness of the problem.

4 With a little intelligence, most risks can be avoided.
5 Our company has a commitment to public safety at all times when people are on our trains.
6 The president had always known about the existence of risks, but chose to ignore this information.
7 The inclusion of reports from several experts gave the paper more authority.

EXTENSION ACTIVITY

1 Write the word *risks* in a circle in the middle of the board. Then create a spider diagram from this word using the following verbs that collocate with *risks*: *avoid, tolerate, anticipate, manage, mitigate*.

2 Check that students understand the verbs (they can use a dictionary if necessary). Drill the verbs, ensuring students are using the correct stress for each: (*avoid, tolerate, anticipate, manage, mitigate*).

3 Ask students to work in pairs to write sentences with these verbs and the word *risks*. Then ask pairs to identify the nouns for each of these verbs (*avoidance, tolerance, anticipation, management, mitigation*). They should then rewrite their sentences, using the nouns rather than the verbs.

4 Invite volunteers to write their noun sentences on the board. Encourage students to provide peer feedback and to correct each others' sentences.

Language development: Possible, probable, and hypothetical future predictions

Refer students to the *Possible, probable, and hypothetical future predictions* box and ask them to read it carefully. Check that they understand the difference between possible, probable, and hypothetical future predictions by asking them to give a percentage for each one based on how likely it is to happen (e.g., probable 80%, possible 30%, hypothetical 2%).

EXTENSION ACTIVITY

Check that students are clear on conditional sentences. Write the following on the board:

A *If I pass my exams, I will go to university.*

B *If I had lots of money, I would buy a sports car.*

Ask students which is a first conditional (A) and which is a second conditional (B). Ask which prediction is more probable (A) and which is more hypothetical (B). Highlight how the sentences are formed (first conditional = present simple + *will*; second conditional = past simple + *would*).

Ask students to rewrite sentence A using *As long as* (As long as I pass my exams, I will go to university.) and sentence B with *Suppose* (Suppose I had lots of money? Then I would buy a sports car.).

1 Remind students to refer back to the table for the language they need to help them complete the sentences. Students can check their answers in pairs before feeding back to the class.

POSSIBLE ANSWERS
1 (unlikely) event (written or spoken)
2 probably/likely (spoken)
3 providing (that) (written or spoken)
4 Even if (written or spoken)
✗ Assuming (that) / As long as / Providing (that) (written or spoken)
6 Suppose / Supposing (spoken)
7 As long as (written or spoken)
8 Unless (spoken)

Even if /
unless

2 Students can stay in their pairs to complete this task. Again, refer them back to the *Possible, probable, and hypothetical future predictions* box to help them. Invite volunteers to write their sentences on the board for analysis.

SPEAKING Undertaking an informal risk assessment

Pronunciation skill

Refer students to the information in the *Word stress in word families* box. Model the pronunciation of the words for the class so that they can hear the word stress.

Remind students to match the words in the box with the rules first, then they can cross out the incorrect options. During class feedback, model the pronunciation of the words and drill them to check students' use of word stress.

ANSWERS
1 destruction; the second to last
2 dangerous; unstressed
3 impossible; unstressed
4 sunglasses; first
5 well-behaved; unstressed

EXTENSION ACTIVITY

Write the following sentences on a sheet of paper, copy it, and cut them up into sentences. Divide your class into pairs and give each pair a set of the four sentences. Ask them to take turns to take a sentence and read it aloud with the correct word stress. Remind them to check the rules they completed in the exercise to help them. Students can correct each other, but monitor and provide input where needed.

1 The infor**ma**tion was a reve**la**tion to the organi**za**tion.
2 The dangers are con**si**derable, **exam**inable, **meas**urable, and under**stand**able.

3 The disre**gard** for safety in this place is unbe**liev**able and il**log**ical.
4 For this as**sign**ment, you need a **lap**top, **note**book, **ball**point pen, and **clip**board.

Speaking skill

Refer students to the *Managing conversation* box and ask them to read it. Highlight the fact that they will need to manage conversations in seminar debates. Allow students to read the phrases and make a note of the use of each one. During class feedback you could drill these phrases to check students' pronunciation and to allow them to become more familiar with these useful language chunks.

ANSWERS
CT: 2, 4, 6, 9
ST: 1, 3, 8, 10
CB: 5, 7

EXTENSION ACTIVITY

Divide the class into groups of three (Student A, Student B, and Student C). Write the following topics on the board: *the weather this week, a country you'd like to visit, a job you'd like to have, a job you'd hate, a sporting event you saw on TV, how your city has changed.*

Then explain these instructions, reminding students to use the phrases for managing conversations:

1 Student A begins talking about one of the topics.
2 Student B listens and interrupts politely, trying to change the topic to something different.
3 Student A continues the conversation and tries to get back to his/her original topic.

Tell Student C to monitor and write down the expressions used so that he/she can then give feedback to others.

SPEAKING TASK

Background information

Formal risk assessment is conducted within many industries, e.g., engineering, nuclear, aerospace, oil. The risk assessment in these situations examines potential hazards, looking at how likely they are to happen, and what the potential losses would be if they did. Risks to human health need to be considered as a priority in all cases. In contrast, with informal risk assessment, the stakes are not so high. Informal risk assessment is used widely in business, especially within project management. This speaking task utilizes informal risk assessment tools, such as risk identification and ways of minimizing risk.

Brainstorm

Put students into groups. Ask them to read the situations and decide together which one they will focus on (or they can create their own if they prefer).

Plan

1 Ask students to work individually to list risks and dangers. Refer them to the ideas in the box to help them, but encourage them to think of their own ideas, too. Ask students to note down their ideas and to write some illustrative sentences to support them. They can look back to page 39 to help them with their illustrative examples.

2 Ask students to continue to work individually at this point, listing risks and suggesting action.

Speak and share

Groups now work together to discuss their ideas. Encourage students to make predictions. Refer them back to the language on page 43 if they need help with this. You should also remind them to use the phrases from page 44 during the conversation. Groups must then agree on the three most important risks and how they will minimize these risks.

Put groups together and ask them to share their risk assessment. Encourage groups to question each other, using language to hypothesize where possible. During this stage, monitor and take language notes. Use the photocopiable *Unit assignment checklist* on page 91 to assess the students' speaking.

Extra research task

Ask students to choose **one** of the following topics to research online:

1 Does gender and age affect a person's willingness to take risks? If so, what reasons are there for this?

2 Are attitudes towards risk-taking linked to nature (personality) or nurture (environment and upbringing)?

Ask them to make notes on their chosen topic. In the next class, group students together according to their chosen topic and ask them to discuss their online research. Encourage them to use the phrases for managing conversations during their discussions.

CRITICAL THINKING SKILLS Knowledge, skills and attitudes

Ask students to complete the self-evaluation questionnaire. They can then read the *Interpreting your score* section. This activity is important as it allows students to assess their own critical thinking skills and reminds them what they need to do in order to raise their skills to the highest possible level.

Cultural awareness

Many of your students may come from cultures where criticizing others and their opinions is seen as impolite. These students do not want to appear disrespectful, but you need to remind them that in western universities it is essential that they do not blindly accept any arguments in an academic context. In western universities they will be expected to analyze, evaluate, and criticize as ways they can fully engage with the academic community and produce meaningful research of their own.

UNIT 5 SPRAWL

Critical thinking	Recognizing logical order Evaluating against criteria
Language development	Connotation Academic verbs
Pronunciation	Contrastive stress
Speaking	Supporting proposals

Discussion point

Direct students' attention to the picture on page 47. Ask them what they can see in the picture (a complex road system, a harbour with boats, trucks with containers, buildings, cars). Brainstorm adjectives students could use to describe the picture, e.g., *industrial, modern, built-up, urban*, etc. Now write the unit title on the board: *sprawl* and explain that it is used as a noun here. Elicit the meaning of the noun (unplanned and uncontrolled spread of urban development). Ask if students think it is a positive or a negative word (negative).

Describe to students an interesting neighborhood that you have visited. If possible, bring in some pictures of the place to show them. Use some of the adjectives from the box in your description and invite questions from students.

Check that students understand the adjectives in the box, then ask pairs to discuss the questions. Once the discussions have finished, invite volunteers to share their ideas with the class.

Vocabulary preview

Write *city infrastructure* on the board. Check that students understand the meaning of the phrase (physical facilities and systems that enable a city to function properly). Ensure that students are also clear on the pronunciation—pay particular attention to the schwa sound in the part of the word in bold: *infrastructure*.

1   Ask students to work individually to complete the table, then compare their answers with a partner.

> **ANSWERS**
> City infrastructure: drainage system, freeway
> Urban issues: urban sprawl, urban decay
> People in the city: pedestrian, merchant
> Places in or around the city: urban block, suburb
> City transportation: trolley, streetcar

2   Ask students to complete the definitions. They can check their answers in pairs before feeding back to the class.

> **ANSWERS**
> 1   freeway   6   pedestrian
> 2   drainage system   7   merchant
> 3   urban decay   8   urban block
> 4   urban sprawl   9   suburb
> 5   trolley; streetcar

EXTENSION ACTIVITY

Write the words from the *Vocabulary preview* section onto cards. Ask students to close their books and work in groups of three. Give a set of cards to each group. Students take turns to take a card and describe the word/phrase on it. The other students in the group have to guess what the word/phrase is.

LISTENING 1 Cars and cities

Before you listen

Ask students to work individually to rank the forms of transportation. Then conduct a class discussion and see if you can collectively agree on a ranking. Encourage students to also consider the environmental impact of these various forms of transportation.

Cultural awareness

In certain cultures, traveling on public transportation is viewed negatively as it is associated with not having your own car, and therefore being poor. This attitude has been prevalent in the U.S., and is only changing now that people are expressing concerns about the environmental impact of private car use.

Listening

Ask students if they know another word for *car*. Elicit *automobile*. Play the audio and ask students to take notes for the dates in the box. Check the answers with the class.

> **AUDIO SCRIPT 1.19**
> **Presenter:** There can be few inventions that we know of today that have transformed the cities as much as the automobile. I say this because in the United States of America, where I'm from, it is currently estimated that almost one half of all land in cities is dedicated, in one way or another, to cars. Streets, roads, parking lots, gas stations, traffic signals, traffic signs, and companies devoted to the automobile industry are such a part of the modern city that we barely notice them.
>
> How did cars take over our cities? Let me give you a clear example. If we look at the history of urban growth

in the United States, we can see that our cities have gradually evolved due to the automobile. Historians divide the late nineteenth and twentieth centuries into three periods. First were the walking cities. This was the model pre-1880. Cities were small and compact, and they featured a mixture of residences and workplaces. People were expected to walk to work, and the rich resided in the center of the cities. This model was the same for many cities around the world that were built more than 200 years ago.

The next key period in the development of transportation in the city lasted between 1880 and 1920. The walking city was superseded by the streetcar city. Cities were feeling the impact of industrialization and the arrival of thousands of immigrants to work in the factories. For instance, the upper classes began to flee the city center to live in newly created suburbs. Cities grew, but around public transportation lines, such as trolleys and streetcars. This period came to an end when the automobile became more and more available.

The automobile's impact was enormous. Let me explain the reasons why I say that. Suddenly people had access, individually, to all kinds of places previously difficult to get to. You could transport yourself and your family wherever you wanted, whenever you wanted. You could access the countryside or go away for the weekend. Most importantly, you didn't need to live close to the place where you worked, so the growth of the suburbs was no longer limited to places served by public transportation. Urban sprawl accelerated rapidly. As more and more individuals bought cars, more and more government policies in urban development began to change.

The automobile, coupled with the arrival of long distance forms of communication, such as the telephone and telegraph, meant that cities could continue to expand and become progressively more decentralized. The suburbs became pushed out further and further. Governments also began to build freeways and highways, great roads that would transport people to and from the workplaces in the city, as well as linking cities with each other. The most famous example of this in American history was the Federal Interstate Highway Act of 1956, which encouraged further urban sprawl across the continent. The automobile had transformed the landscape into real estate. Empty land, now connected by roads and cars, could gain value and be sold.

For the rest of the twentieth century, the automobile continued to dominate urban growth, both in the United States, but also arguably around the world. However, in the face of worsening traffic congestion, urban decay, lack of efficient public transportation, and the scarcity of oil we have to urgently reconsider our relationship with cars.

The European Union, in a 2011 White Paper on transportation, revealed that they wanted to eliminate conventionally-fueled cars from all cities by 2050. It is commonly understood that people would have to rely on electric cars, or on public transportation. Moves such as these and others around the world suggest that we may be about to shift towards a fourth type of city, the post-automobile city.

The post-automobile city is not car-free, but is redesigned to offer infrastructure for pedestrians and those who desire to live without cars. There are more parks, gardens, pathways, pedestrian shopping streets, and bicycle lanes. Such a vision is already becoming a reality in many cities. That is where I wish to turn my attention next …

POSSIBLE ANSWERS

Pre-1880	• Cities were walking cities. • They were small and compact. • They had a mixture of residences and workplaces. • The rich resided in the center of the cities.
1880–1920	• Cities became known as streetcar cities. • Upper classes left the city center to live in the suburbs. • Cities grew around public transportation lines, such as trolleys and streetcars.
Post-1920	• People had individual access to all kinds of places previously difficult to get to. • Families could transport themselves wherever and whenever they wanted to. • They could access the countryside or go away for the weekend. • People didn't need to live close to the place where they worked. • Government policies in urban development began to change. • Cities continued to grow. • Governments also began to build freeways and highways.
2011	• The European Union wanted to eliminate conventionally-fueled cars from all cities by 2050. • People would have to rely on electric cars, or on public transportation. • We may be about to see the beginning of a fourth type of city, the post-automobile city.

walk

public transport

car

Refer students to the *Academic keywords* box and check their pronunciation of the words. Ensure that they are clear on the meanings. Ask them to check in their dictionaries if they are unsure.

EXTENSION ACTIVITY

Write the following information on the board: *Are Americans falling out of love with the automobile? Since the year 2000, total vehicle miles traveled in cars in the U.S. has been falling.* Ask students to work in small groups to discuss this information and to think of reasons why it might be happening. After a few minutes, open this up to a class discussion. Reasons include an increase in internet shopping, homeworking, increased costs for young people buying cars, more awareness of environmental impact. Ask students whether this trend is also occurring in their own countries. Why or why not?

Critical thinking skill

Refer students to the *Recognizing logical order* box and ask them to read the information carefully.

SUPPORTING CRITICAL THINKING

Ask students if they are able to concentrate for an entire lecture. The answer will most likely be *no*. It is hard for any student to concentrate for that length of time and is even more difficult for non-native speakers, so it is highly likely students will miss some of the information given. This is where being able to recognize logical order can help as it can enable students to fill in any gaps in their notes.

1 Allow plenty of time for students to read the statements. They can then decide which information should follow. Don't go over the answers at this stage.

ANSWERS
1 a   2 b   3 b

2 Remind students that they don't have to use the exact words that were in the audio, as long as the meaning is the same. Again, don't check the answers.

POSSIBLE ANSWERS
1 offices/companies/workplaces
2 large roads/highways
3 stop/reduce; cars/transportation

3 Play the audio so students can check their answers to exercises 1 and 2.

Developing critical thinking

Ask students to work in groups and discuss the questions. Circulate and monitor, noting any interesting arguments and any language errors for feedback.

EXTENSION ACTIVITY

Tell the class that they work for a city council and they must reduce the number of cars being used in the city center. Divide the class into two groups: Group A and Group B. Write the following on the board:

Group A: *Your solution is to make using a car in the city center difficult and expensive.*

Group B: *Your solution is to make using public transportation, bicycles, or walking in the city center more appealing.*

Ask each group to prepare their arguments. They should think of how they will put their plan into action (e.g., Group A: high parking costs, one-way streets, congestion charges; Group B: cheap and frequent buses or trams, cycle lanes, pedestrianized areas).

The groups should debate the issue and try to reach an agreement. They should consider the costs, the popularity of the idea, and the practicalities.

LISTENING 2 Making cities more liveable *all women again!*

Before you listen

1 Check students understand the word *liveable* (being a good place to live with a high quality of life). Allow students time to consider the importance of the listed factors and to come up with two of their own.

2 Remind students to compare their answers and explain their reasons to their partner.

Listening

Before they listen, refer students to the *Academic keywords* box. Check they understand the words and that they can pronounce them correctly. Ask them to use their dictionaries if they are unsure on meaning. Highlight the fact that *criterion* is more often seen in the plural form (*criteria*).

Ask students to read the definitions. Check they understand the words *resilience* (the ability to tolerate stress and to recover quickly from problems), *capacity* (ability), *integrated* (unified—when all parts come together), and *residents* (people who live in a certain place). Then play the audio so that students can match the criteria with the definitions. Check answers with the class.

AUDIO SCRIPT   1.20
Podcaster: The world's population is rising at an increasingly rapid pace. According to a recent United Nations population publication, two thirds of our planet's inhabitants will live in cities by the year 2050. This fast-paced urbanisation around the globe produces both social and environmental challenges for city planners. In the first of our course podcasts during the second semester we are going to focus on the term *liveable cities*. We have invited representatives from two cities that have entered this year's Philips Liveable Cities Award. Unlike some liveability ranking data this award doesn't focus on salaries, it focuses on well-being. This contest will reward the most innovative and feasible ideas for improving the health and well-being of people living in cities. Let me explain the criteria for this competition. According to the Philips Think Tank there are three vital ingredients of a liveable city. The first is Resilience—this refers to a city's ability to adapt to the requirements of its citizens. The second ingredient is Inclusiveness, which describes the city's ability to generate a community in all sections of the population regardless of gender, age, or ethnicity. The final element is Authenticity. This refers to the city's character and identity.

ANSWERS
1 c   2 a   3 b

Critical thinking skill

Ask students to read the information in the *Evaluating against criteria* box carefully. Highlight that it is essential to know what the criteria are before you evaluate an idea. If you used the *Extension activity* at the end of *Listening 1*, remind students of it and explain that their evaluation of the different suggestions changed according to their criteria (e.g., if cost is the most important criterion, then increased parking costs is a better option than cheaper public transport, but if popularity with residents is more important, the opposite is true).

1 Ask students to read the table carefully, then play part 2 so that students can take notes. Students can then compare their notes in pairs.

AUDIO SCRIPT 1.21

Podcaster: So, to talk to you about what projects these two cities are developing this year, I'd like to welcome Maja Jorgenson from Copenhagen in Denmark and Adhira Joshi from New Delhi in India.

Maja and Adhira: Hello.

Podcaster: Good afternoon to you both. Thanks for coming along to talk to us. Maja, could you start by telling us about Copenhagen's contribution to their citizens' health and well-being?

Maja: Hello. Yes, certainly. In Copenhagen we feel that urban planners have to adapt to the needs of the people. So, we believe in involving our citizens in the decision-making that will mould our city's future by consulting them as part of the urban development process. Inclusiveness is a vital part of making a city more liveable. This method allows us to see what people expect from our planners. We also believe that it helps residents feel that they can help mould the present and the future of the city.

So, what do people expect? Well, first of all, we now know that there is an overall acceptance that good quality architecture should always be an integral part of city planning. This gives people a certain feeling of pride in Copenhagen's identity.

Our current city planning isn't only about architecture; it also includes green spaces. We know that if we make the city green, with gardens, parks, and trees, it will make it an attractive place, a place where people will want to stay, and not seek to escape. Rather than go outside in search of nature, people can find it right on their doorstep.

A sense of community is very important to us, so we feel that where necessary we have to introduce new ways of fostering this. Part of our recent success is integrating community functions by bringing public life into the building. We have created urban blocks that act as small communities by mixing all the different functions together: the living spaces, parks, retail areas, and leisure spaces are all assimilated into the design of the building. This gives people the opportunity to come together and enjoy their lives close to home. Moving all these elements closer together also means we can actually keep population density low and create a sense of community among our citizens.

Another issue we have had to deal with is the seasonal variations in daylight because of Denmark's northern location. There are very short days during winter as well as very long summer days. Our aim is to enhance people's lives by varying the type and amount of lighting from the dark autumn months to the longer and darker winter months.

We have invested heavily in city lighting to satisfy our citizens' physical, social, and psychological needs. We believe cities should be provided with light when it is needed; we want residents to use the city at night. Well-lit environments foster creativity, social activity, and help build strong communities. It also cultivates a sense of trust and safety, which is a vital factor for people to have the freedom to enjoy our city.

---

2 Play part 3. Again, allow students to compare their notes in pairs before feeding back to the class.

AUDIO SCRIPT 2.01

Podcaster: Thank you, Maja. I'm now going to ask Adhira to speak about a rather different set of urban issues that India's largest city, New Delhi is striving to deal with.

Adhira: Hi, there. Yes, New Delhi isn't India's largest city; it's the largest metropolitan area in India. It's what we call a mega city, which means a city with a population in excess of ten million. We actually have 23 million. So as you can see, it's a populous city. It has been said that mega cities bring mega problems, and traffic is certainly one of the biggest challenges we face in New Delhi as regards quality of life. We are currently working on a scheme to reduce the amount of traffic in the centre and bring our citizens back to a part of the city, rich in heritage, which has been lost because of the city's road system.

One thing we are looking at is parks. Parks are vital to the city's resilience; they are the lungs of New Delhi, and this is vital in an environmental sense. If parks are the lungs, then water is the blood of a city! Another plan is to rejuvenate an ancient drainage system that will fill the dry canals with water, and develop these canals into public areas, for example, walkways and cycle paths for people to enjoy their city more peacefully.

At the heart of the development of social spaces is the concept of inclusion. We want to provide a refuge for people from all walks of life; these are spaces for everyone, and everyone should be able to afford the activities being planned for these areas.

Commerce is also an important aspect in every city. In New Delhi our street traders add vibrancy to the neighbourhoods, and this is something we aim to encourage. We have made ample space for this activity and reduced the cost of rent for our merchants. People walking home at night feel much more secure in lively streets full of commercial activity. It helps create a safe and close community.

We also really want to encourage civic pride in New Delhi, and promoting heritage can be one way of doing it. One of our latest projects is the Guru Tegh Bahadur memorial, which is a new public area dedicated to the great Sikh gurus. This is truly a place for the people who can have the dual experience of relaxing around the central tower in a much-needed, green public space while contemplating the teachings of the gurus that are engraved on huge monoliths placed in a circle around them.

Podcaster: Thank you, Adhira. Well, as we have heard, two different cities on opposite sides of the world with one common aim: Making their city more liveable.

ANSWERS

Criteria	Copenhagen	New Delhi
Resilience	Current planning includes green spaces such as parks, gardens, and trees. Lighting has been invested in as a well-lit environment fosters creativity and social activity.	A plan to bring the citizens back into the city centre. Reduce the amount of traffic in the centre to build new parks.
Inclusiveness	Part of the urban development process includes consultation with residents. Projects create a sense of community for residents.	Develop new public areas. Rejuvenating canals and building walkways and cycle paths. They want to include people from all walks of life. It will not be too expensive for anyone.
Authenticity	Good quality architecture gives people a sense of pride in the city.	Encouraging civic pride by promoting heritage. The building of the Guru Tegh Bahadur memorial. The teachings of the gurus are engraved on huge monoliths in the park.

3   Allow students time to discuss their ideas with their partner, then invite volunteers to share their thoughts with the class.

Developing critical thinking

1   Put students into small groups to discuss the questions.

2   Remind students to also think back to the listening text *Cars and cities* before they discuss these questions.

Language development: Connotation

Refer students to the *Connotation* box and ask them to read it carefully. Highlight the fact that a speaker can show his/her feelings about an issue simply through the words he/she chooses. Remind them of the unit title, *Sprawl*. Can they remember whether this word has positive or negative connotations (negative)?

1   Encourage students to use their dictionaries if they are struggling, as there are often clues in the definitions (e.g., *sprawl* is defined as a large area of buildings that are spread out in an unattractive way, so the word *unattractive* highlights negative connotations). Once they have decided on the connotations, they can then choose the odd word out in each set. Allow students to check their answers in pairs before feeding back to the class.

ANSWERS

1   cramped –, populous ≈, overcrowded – (different connotation: populous)
2   reckon ≈, contemplate ≈, reflect ≈ (different connotation: reckon)
3   growth ≈, expansion ≈, sprawl – (different connotation: sprawl)
4   struggle –, strive +, endeavor + (different connotation: struggle)
5   ample +, enough ≈, abundant + (different connotation: enough)
6   push out –, expand ≈, extend ≈ (different connotation: push out)

2   Remind students to look for clues in the sentences to show whether the speaker is feeling positive or negative. Students may need to refer to their dictionaries for help with some of the words.

ANSWERS
1 c   2 b   3 a   4 a   5 c

Language development: Academic verbs

Refer students to the *Academic verbs* box and ask them to read it carefully. Highlight that students need to be careful when using synonyms for academic verbs, as there are often subtle differences in meaning.

1   This exercise highlights the differences in meaning with academic verbs. Encourage students to attempt this exercise without referring to a dictionary—they can use context to help them. Then check their answers in pairs before feeding back to the class.

ANSWERS
1 c   2 f   3 a   4 d   5 b   6 e

2 Write the verbs on the board: *shift, vary, transform, develop, evolve, adapt.* Ask students to close their books before they start to test each other. They can refer back to page 53 if they are struggling.

POSSIBLE ANSWERS

shift: consciously change your way of thinking
vary: make changes in something in order to give more diversity
transform: make something or someone completely different
develop: change land for a particular purpose
evolve: progressively change over a period of time
adapt: change your ideas or behavior so that you can deal with a new situation

---

3 Ask students to complete the sentences individually. Check answers with the class.

ANSWERS

1 vary	3 evolved
2 adapt	4 transformed

EXTENSION ACTIVITY

Remind students they have been looking at verbs associated with change. Now ask them to focus on six verbs associated with getting something. Write the following verbs on the board: *acquire, obtain, gain, receive, incur, inherit.* Ask them to work in pairs to research these verbs. They should use their dictionaries to find the following: pronunciation, meaning, an example sentence.

Ask them to make a note of their findings. They should then work together to create their own example sentences for the six verbs. Circulate and check their sentences, or collect them in for correction if you prefer.

This is a good place to use the video resource *The urban footprint.* It is located in the Video resources section of the digital component. Alternatively, remind students about the video so they can do this at home.

SPEAKING Presenting a proposal of an action plan for an urban issue

Pronunciation skill

Refer students to the *Contrastive stress* box and ask them to read it carefully. Highlight that the stress is used on nouns, noun phrases, and gerund phrases in these examples.

1 Ask students to underline the words they think will be stressed.

2 Play the audio for students to check their answers.

AUDIO SCRIPT 2.02

1
Maja: Our current city planning isn't only about architecture; it also includes green spaces.

2
Adhira: New Delhi isn't India's largest city; it's the largest metropolitan area.

3
Adhira: If parks are the lungs, then water is the blood of a city!

ANSWERS

1 Our current city planning isn't only about **architecture**; it also includes **green spaces**.
2 New Delhi isn't India's largest **city**; it's the largest **metropolitan area**.
3 If parks are the **lungs**, then water is the **blood** of a city!

---

3 Alert students to the fact that this task will involve fairly basic sentences, but that the point is to practice word stress in their pronunciation. Before students write sentences about their partner, demonstrate the task by writing untrue sentences about yourself on the board (e.g., *I come from France. I live in a large house.*). Now use contrastive stress to correct them (e.g., *I don't come from France, I come from America. I don't live in a large house, I live in a small apartment.*). Monitor whilst students correct the sentences, checking that they are using contrastive stress.

Speaking skill

Refer students to the *Supporting proposals* box and ask them to read it carefully. Remind them that if they want to persuade their audience to agree with a proposal, they must give reasons and examples.

1 Play the audio. Students note down the problems and solutions. Check answers with the class.

AUDIO SCRIPT 2.03

Common sense tells us that more people will use the subway if we make it more easily accessible. For instance, taking a bus means we will definitely be there before it starts.

It just makes sense to increase fares. The service has been suffering from a lack of funding for years.

We have to consider a one-ticket system for all the services. I say this because I feel that, this way, more people will use public transportation.

ANSWERS

1 Problem: Few people travel by subway due to limited accessibility.

Solution: Make the subway more accessible.

2 Problem: If they don't, they may arrive late.

Solution: Go to the event by bus.

3 Problem: The service is suffering from financial problems.

Solution: Increase the price of public transportation.

4 Problem: Not enough people are traveling by public transportation.

Solution: Introduce one ticket for all modes of public transportation.

2 Ask students to work with a partner. Remind them to use language from the *Supporting proposals* box during their discussions. Circulate and monitor, making a note of any language points for feedback.

SPEAKING TASK

Brainstorm and plan

Ask students to work in pairs to brainstorm their ideas. Encourage them to add reasons, evidence, and examples to their list.

Write the following table on the board and ask students to copy it into their notebooks. Remind students to choose just one of the problems from the *Brainstorm* section. They should then complete their table.

The problem	Effects of the problem	Solution	Reasons and evidence for solution

Speak and share

Before you group pairs together for this task, ask them to look back at the key language points in the unit and to make a note of any language they would like to use when they present their proposal. Now ask pairs to come together with other pairs who chose the same problem. Encourage students to ask each other questions. Circulate and monitor, paying particular attention to the use of language students practiced in the unit.

Discuss the proposed solutions with the whole class and encourage peer feedback. Then provide any feedback of your own. Decide on the most effective proposals. During this stage, monitor and take language notes. Use the photocopiable *Unit assignment checklist* on page 92 to assess the students' speaking.

Extra research task

Ask students to research one of the following real-life urban problems online (or they can choose another example if they prefer):

1 Pollution in a large city in your country.

2 Traffic in your capital city.

They should prepare a short presentation for the next class covering the areas from the speaking task (the problem, the effects of the problem, a proposed solution with reasons and evidence).

STUDY SKILLS Recording achievement

Getting started

After pairs have discussed the questions, open this up to the class. Remind students that identifying their own academic successes and understanding why they did well can help them continue to achieve.

Scenario

Ask students to read about Kyung-mi and make a list of information that could be included in a personal portfolio. Students can compare their ideas in pairs before feeding back to the class.

POSSIBLE ANSWER

I might include a monthly schedule of my activities. I would keep track of events that I have participated in, whether they are academic or non-academic, and reflect on how they may have contributed to my overall personal development. I might also include an emotions diary and see how my mood affected my productivity. I also might include essay drafts and compare how my thought processes change across an assignment.

Consider it

Allow time for students to read the tips, then open this up to the whole class and find out which tips are most commonly used.

Over to you

Refer students back to the tips before they begin their discussion. During class feedback challenge the students to try one of the tips over the next week.

Critical thinking	Source validity Use of the passive in source citations
Language development	Inversion Collocations: *way*
Pronunciation	Pausing for dramatic emphasis
Speaking	Emphasizing important information—repetition and contrastive pairs

Discussion point

Direct students' attention to the picture on page 57. Ask them if they know where the picture was taken (Petra, Jordan). Ask what they know about Petra.

Background information

Petra is a vast historical city in Jordan carved into a rock face and is thought to date back to 312 BC. It was the capital city of an ancient people, known as the Nabataeans. Today, Petra is a UNESCO World Heritage Site.

Ask students if they understand the word *legacy*. Explain that it describes a gift passed on from people in the past. This gift can be something physical, as in the city of Petra passed on by the Nabataeans, or it can be intangible, such as a skill or a way of thinking.

Direct students' attention to the discussion questions and the quotations. Ask them to read the quotes carefully and check they understand them. Explain that *would not* in the second quote is a literary way of saying *don't want to*. Have pairs discuss the questions, then invite students to share their ideas with the class.

Vocabulary preview

1 Encourage students to do this exercise without dictionaries. They can discuss their ideas in pairs before feeding back to the class.

ANSWERS
1 launch, unveiling
2 to revolutionize, to change the face of
3 to address, to deal with
4 to hand down, to pass on
5 achievement, success
6 to convey, to express
7 to stand to, to be likely to
8 ritual, custom

2 Remind students about connotation, i.e., that a word can have certain positive or negative associations. Help students to get started by looking at the difference between *launch* and *unveiling* together (refer to the answer key). Then ask

them to work together to examine the remaining synonyms.

POSSIBLE ANSWERS
1 *launch* might suggest more power and energy behind revealing a new product or idea to an audience; *unveiling* suggests some surprise behind the object to be revealed
2 *to revolutionize* suggests a more radical and rapid process of change than *to change the face of*
3 *to address* is a more formal synonym of *to deal with*
4 *to hand down* is more often used to refer to transmitting something across generations or across ranks
5 an *achievement* might not result in success in terms of winning or being better than someone else, but could be a comparative or benchmarking accomplishment, such as someone who had lost the capacity to walk being able to stand up and take a few steps
6 *to express* sounds more forceful and direct than *to convey*; *convey* might be closer to the meaning of *to suggest*
7 *to be likely to* suggests a probability; *to stand to* suggests that a condition must be met first before the probability becomes likely
8 a *custom* is an action or practice that has become a general habit among a specific group of people, such as giving flowers on Mother's Day; a *ritual* can heavily overlap the usage of *custom*, but implies that there are often more stages in the process, such as superstitious practices that some athletes might go through before a key event

3 Tell students that the numbers of this exercise correlate with the numbers in exercise 1. Students work individually. They can then check their answers in pairs before feeding back to the class.

ANSWERS
1 launch
2 revolutionized / changed the face of
3 address / deal with
4 handed down / passed on
5 success / achievement
6 convey / express
7 stand to / are likely to
8 customs

4 Ask students to discuss whether they agree with the statements or not in pairs. Then invite volunteers to share their ideas with the class.

LISTENING 1 Family food legacies

Before you listen

Allow time for students to discuss the questions in pairs before opening this up to a class discussion.

Cultural awareness

The importance of food and eating together varies greatly between cultures. In some cultures, even a common greeting is connected with food, e.g., in Chinese it is common to greet people with the phrase *Have you eaten?* In many cultures, people also pride themselves on offering hospitality to guests or strangers by inviting them to a meal.

In many industrialized nations, it has become more common for people to eat alone and to eat quickly since other activities have become more important. However, even in some European cultures, eating still has real significance, and in countries such as France and Italy people often get together to enjoy a long meal together.

Listening

1 Refer students to the mind map, then play the audio while they listen and take notes.

AUDIO SCRIPT 2.04

Lecturer: Hi everyone and welcome back to our family studies course. Last week I promised we would address the issue of food traditions and legacies in family units. I asked you all to write about some kind of food-related tradition that you have experienced in your family and to upload it to our course forum. I wanted to address this whole area a bit more in today's class.

Thank you so much for your varied responses. I can see that many of you have rich and delicious memories relating to the family table. Before we look at specific examples, I thought it might be worthwhile to go over some of the theory and research that has gone on in this area.

First of all, by family food legacy I meant something food-related that comes from the past or that happened in the past. This could be a special dish or recipe that is handed down from generation to generation. Or perhaps a family ritual that is connected in some way to food or mealtimes. Barbara Feise and her colleagues at the University of Illinois make the distinction between family routines and family rituals in their analysis of 17 previous studies on weight, food consumption, and eating habits. The study sample took in the family eating routines of 182,000 children and adolescents. A family routine typically involves communication about something that needs to be done. Once the act is completed it is not really thought about. For example, a food-related routine might involve clearing the plates from the table or picking up bread from the bakery. These routines are repeated over time and become habits, but do not have deep symbolism.

A family ritual, on the other hand, involves communication of a more symbolic nature. According to a number of reports, not only does a ritual convey a sense of who we are as a group, but it also makes the family feel like they belong together. For example, a family mealtime ritual could be a symbolic act, it could involve objects, or it could be conversations. These do not have to be large or extreme. It could be as simple as a joke about who finishes their food first or who says what at the table. It could be a dish that the family eats on special occasions or a moment of silence before a meal that everyone respects. It could be the same repeated subjects of conversation that only occur at the dinner table. When a family ritual is passed down through generations it becomes a legacy. Only when the rituals occupy an important part in each individual's mind do they give the family its own meaning.

And the family mealtime ritual has been the subject of great interest in the social sciences. There is something about what happens when people share a meal that brings the family group together. Sharing of food is a deeply human instinct in all cultures, a point drawn out in Russell Belk's recent article "Sharing," from the Journal of Consumer Research published by The University of Chicago Press. Belk draws attention to the similar patterns of sharing on all continents. During family mealtimes, legends are passed down, jokes are told, and the wider world is eventually examined through the family's own values. This strengthens the family connection; it strengthens the family identity.

And it's good for us in other ways. Various studies across North America and the United Kingdom show that the more often families eat together, the more likely children are to have confidence in themselves. Children who eat regular meals with their parents were found to be 40% more likely to score good grades and felt that their parents were proud of them. Robin Fox, an American anthropologist who teaches at Rutgers University in New Jersey, says that a meal is more than just about the food. It's about civilizing people, about teaching them to be members of our culture.

And yet, many argue that this kind of ritual is in decline. According to the American Institute of Pediatrics, conflicting work schedules, lack of commitment, interference of television, and food-related problems such as lack of cooking skills have all led to the family meal becoming less and less common. If we look at the statistics in three countries: Britain, Canada, and the U.S., we see that less than half of all families with children eat dinner together at home every day.

What does the decline of families sharing mealtimes together mean for future generations? What are the social implications and what do we stand to lose when we stop eating together? I began this lecture explaining what I meant by a food legacy: something that comes from the past, that is handed down to us from the past, or that happens in the past. Before we go back to your great entries on the forum of your own food-related memories I'd like you to reflect on one question. What food legacy do you want to leave your children?

POSSIBLE ANSWERS

Reasons for the decline in sharing meals: *conflicting work schedules, lack of commitment, interference of television, and lack of cooking skills*

What can happen when people share a meal?: *legends are passed down, jokes are told, and the wider world is examined through the family's own values*

Examples of family food legacies: *a special dish or recipe that is handed down from generation to generation, a family ritual that is connected in some way to food or mealtimes*

The positive effects of sharing a meal: *children are more likely to have confidence in themselves, to score good grades, and to feel that their parents are proud of them*

2 Students compare their mind maps in pairs before feeding back to the class.

Refer students to the *Academic keywords* box. Check that they can pronounce the words correctly and that they are clear on the meanings.

Critical thinking skill

Ask students to read the information in the *Source validity* box. Highlight that it is important to use reliable sources when conducting research, so they must always question the reliability of what they read. Remind students to always make a note of the source for their bibliographies before they take quotes, as it is harder to find this information retrospectively.

1 Ask students to read the table so they are clear what information is missing. Then play the audio for them to complete the table. They can then compare their answers with a partner before feeding back to the class.

2 Discuss these questions as a class. Remind students that primary sources, such as the class online forum, can be interesting but are often unreliable as they only examine a small number of people. Students should be able to fill in some of the gaps by searching on a library database.

Developing critical thinking

Ask students to discuss the questions in groups. Circulate and note any interesting ideas that can be shared with the class as a follow-up.

POSSIBLE ANSWERS

Information	Source name	Publication name	Primary (P) / Secondary (S) source?	Authoritative source?	Valid research participant base?
A meal is more than just about food—it's about civilizing people.	Robin Fox	n/a	S	✓ Anthropologist at Rutgers University, U.S.	n/a
A family routine involves discussion about a task.	Barbara Feise et al.	n/a	S	✓ University of Illinois, U.S.	✓ 182,000 youngsters
There are similar patterns of sharing ideas at the dinner table across countries.	Russell Belk	"Sharing," Journal of Consumer Research, UoC Press	S	n/a	n/a
Rich and delicious memories connected to eating at home.	The class in the audio track lecture	Online forum	P	no	n/a
A ritual makes a family feel united.	n/a	Some reports	S	n/a	n/a

LISTENING 2 Technology legacies

Before you listen

1 Ask students to discuss their opinions in pairs before sharing ideas with the class.

2 Discuss these questions with the class. You may like to provide more information using the *Background information* box.

Background information

Konrad Zuse finished his Z3 computer in 1941 in Germany. Among the first computers was the Commodore PET, released in the U.S. in 1977.

The Internet developed with the arrival of the computer, although there was a pre-cursory concept called the noosphere, from Vernadsky, de Chardin, and Le Roy. In the noosphere, humans can connect to an interconnected network of resources.

The term "smartphone" was first used in 1997, by the Swedish company, Ericsson.

Tablet computers have been marketed since the 1990s, and the most famous is the Apple® iPad, released in 2010.

3 Ask students to identify the people in the pictures. They have all been innovators in computing technology.

ANSWERS

a Tim Berners-Lee (inventor of the World Wide Web; British, b. 1955)

b Steve Jobs (co-founder of Apple Inc.; American, 1955–2011)

c Alan Turing (early computer scientist who developed computer programs; British, 1912–1954)

Listening

Play the audio and ask students to complete the information. Check answers as a class. *All girls again*

AUDIO SCRIPT 2.05

Student A: So, I thought maybe we could start with my choice since it's the most up to date and still current in everyone's minds.

Student B: OK, who's that?

Student A: Steve Jobs.

Student B: Well, it's certainly current. But why him?

Student A: Where do you want me to start? Creates the Macintosh computer for Apple® in 1984. Leaves Apple® and returns, releasing the new iMac® computer in 1998. Creates the iPod music player in 2001. Starts iTunes in 2003, changing the way music is sold online. 2007 sees the launch of iPhone. Then we've got a few versions of the iPhone, the iPod and so on until, until 2010 when

the iPad is launched. By this point Apple® is one of the biggest companies in the world.

Student C: These are just products and dates, though. Remember the focus has to be on how significant the impact of his work has been. You'd need more details on why these achievements exactly—the technological ones—have created a lasting legacy.

Student A: I think you could argue that Apple® changed the face of modern computing. Without Apple, there would not have been Windows. Before the Macintosh computer I think that computing was the domain of ... of academics and scientists.

Student B: So, how exactly? Specifically?

Student A: It's been argued that Apple® and Steve Jobs were responsible for bringing computer icons and the mouse to a greater public. Therefore, both of these made the use of computers a lot easier. Plus we have the introduction of the iPod, which transformed the music industry. There are more, let's see—the launch of the iPhone revolutionized the phone industry. Err ... they were the first to introduce the tablet computer ... the iPad, thus creating the tablet industry. But I'd focus more on the transformation of computers from a business machine to a machine for the wider public as his main legacy. Anyway, enough about mine. What about each of you?

Student B: Well, mine isn't as contemporary, but I've chosen Alan Turing. You could argue that without Turing, Steve Jobs wouldn't have had a job.

Student A: OK, go on.

Student B: Turing is considered the father of modern computing. He was a mathematician at Cambridge who, at 23, created a machine which was set up to read and write numbers, and do some simple functions. This was way back in 1937. This machine, the Universal Turing machine, in principle could calculate all the things that were possible in mathematics. Then he also became well known for his work during World War II, working on developing computers that could break German codes.

Student C: So what was his legacy? Why would he be someone on the list?

Student B: Well, there were no computers before then at all really. So, this was a very important first step in the world of modern computing. I also read that Turing computers are still an essential element even today in the study of the theory of computing. And he had a test named after him, the Turing test, which measures artificial intelligence and is still widely used today.

Student A: OK, sounds good. So to summarize his legacy it would be ...

Student B: Well, he developed the FIRST computer. Sure, it was the size of a room and today's tablets can fit in your pocket, but still, it's pretty impressive.

Student C: OK, can I tell you about mine now?

Student C: I chose Tim Berners-Lee.

Student A & B: Mmmm. OK. The inventor of the Internet.

Student C: Yeah. Of all the claims to leaving a legacy, inventing the World Wide Web has got to be the best. Umm ... Berners-Lee was born in 1955.

Student A: Best to stick to his achievements and how they left a lasting legacy in the world of computing …

Student C: OK, OK. In the 1980s, while working at CERN (the European Organization for Nuclear Research) Tim Berners-Lee decides to experiment with a system to share and update information between researchers called ENQUIRE. The system used hypertext to send the information. Later, in 1989, Berners-Lee sees the opportunity to link hypertext to the Internet which, at the time, was only a way of connecting computer networks across the world. As a result, the World Wide Web was born. Berners-Lee is credited also with building the first web browser, creating the first web server, and …

Student B: And so changing the world as we know it.

Student C: Of course. We are all so reliant now on the Internet that it's impossible to imagine life without the World Wide Web. Not only did it revolutionize how we communicate with each other, but also how we access and spread information.

Student A: So. The man who invented the first computer, the creator of the Internet, and the contributions of Apple® to the world of computing. We're down to three from our original eight … I guess next we can put each into a slideshow and maybe ask the class to say which they think had the MOST important effect.

ANSWERS

Student 1: Steve Jobs; Apple changed the face of modern computing.
Student 2: Alan Turing; He developed the first computer.
Student 3: Tim Berners-Lee; He invented the World Wide Web.

Ask students to look at the *Academic keywords* box. Check that they can pronounce the words correctly and are clear on the meanings. Again, you could extend this by asking them to brainstorm the word families, e.g., *contribute* (v), *contributing* (adj).

Critical thinking skill

Ask students to read the *Use of the passive in source citations* box. Remind them that they can use the passive in their academic work, but should follow up with more concrete information, e.g., *It is thought that …, and/but Barnes (2009) states that …*

1 Play the audio again and ask students to complete the table. You may need to pause or play relevant sections again to allow students to make notes.

ANSWERS

Inventor	A citation that uses a passive construction
Apple®/Steve Jobs	It's been argued that Apple® and Steve Jobs were responsible for bringing computer icons and the mouse to a greater public.
Alan Turing	Turing is considered the father of modern computing.
Tim Berners-Lee	Berners-Lee is credited also with building the first web browser, creating the first web server, and …

2 Students rephrase the citations individually. They can then compare their ideas with a partner before feeding back to the class.

POSSIBLE ANSWERS

1 According to Volume 8 of the *Electro Academia, Times Journal*, Apple and Steve Jobs were responsible for bringing computer icons and the mouse to a greater public.

2 Leading computer historians Smith and Perez consider Turing the father of modern computing.

3 Thomas, professor of Information Technology from Bright University, in her 2008 book *Http*, credits Berners-Lee with building the first web browser and creating the first web server.

Developing critical thinking

1 Ask students to work in groups to discuss the questions. Circulate and note any interesting comments.

2 Ask students to discuss these questions in groups. Invite volunteers to share their ideas with the class.

Language development: Inversion

Refer students to the *Inversion* box and ask them to read it carefully. Alert them to the change in word order when these techniques are used. Encourage them to choose some of the examples given and make an effort to incorporate them into their own work when they want to create emphasis, as this will add a degree of sophistication to their writing and speaking.

1 Students complete the sentences individually. Remind them to look back at the examples in the *Inversion* box if they are struggling.

ANSWERS

1 only 2 no 3 Never 4 now 5 sooner

2 Students can check their rewritten sentences in pairs before feeding back to the class.

ANSWERS

1 Never again will there be a technological revolution.
2 Not only did Apple® revolutionize the phone industry, but they also created the tablet industry.
3 No sooner do phone companies release the latest model than they bring a newer one out.
4 Not until Microsoft® Windows was launched were computers available to the general public.
5 Rarely do you meet anyone nowadays who doesn't have a computer.
6 Only by reading their biography and using their product can you understand someone's technological legacy.
7 Only recently has my family started to pass on family mealtime rituals.

This is a good place to use the video resource *Tracing the family line*. It is located in the Video resources section of the digital component.

Language development: Collocations: *way*

Ask students to read the information in the *Collocations: way* box. Remind them that learning how words collocate can really help to improve their language fluency. Encourage them to note common collocations whenever they record a new word.

1 Ask students to complete the sentences. They can then check their answers in pairs. Note that for question 5, *in a bad way* is typically a British English expression. Americans would more likely say *in bad shape*.

ANSWERS

1 on	5 in
2 long	6 give
3 into	7 have
4 go	8 toward

2 Ask students to match the collocations with their definitions. Check the answers with the class.

ANSWERS

a have a way with	e a long way
b give way to	f in a bad way
c on its way	g way into
d went a long way toward	h the way to go

3 Discuss these questions as a class. Refer students back to the sentences in exercise 1 to help them

make a decision about formality. They should conclude that *on its way, the way to go, in a bad way, have a way with* are more informal. The other expressions could be more safely used in formal speaking and writing.

ANSWERS

1, 4, 5, 6, and 7 are the most informal.
2, 3, and 8 could be used in more formal settings.

4 In each pair, one student should close their book while their partner tests them. They then swap roles.

EXTENSION ACTIVITY

Write the following sentence from the audio on the board and underline *first step: This was a very important first step in the world of modern computing.*

Ask students to work in pairs to brainstorm as many collocations with the word *step* as they can. They can use their dictionaries to help them. Then ask students to note the meanings of the collocations they have listed and whether they can be used in formal speaking/ writing. Possibilities include: VERB *to step down, to step it up, to step up to the plate, to step into someone's shoes, to step out with someone;* NOUN *a step forward, a step backward, a step too far, a sideways step.*

SPEAKING Making a speech about a person who has left a legacy

Pronunciation skill

Ask students to read the information in the *Pausing for dramatic emphasis* box. Highlight the connection between punctuation and pauses. Remind students that integrating pauses into their presentations can really assist their audience and can help retain their attention.

1 Students should mark where they think the pauses should be.

2 Play the audio so students can check their answers.

AUDIO SCRIPT 2.06

1 A family mealtime ritual could be a symbolic act; // it could involve objects, // or it could be conversations.
2 Sure, it was the size of a room, // and today's tablets can fit in your pocket, // but still, it's pretty impressive.
3 No sooner do phone companies release the latest model // than a newer one comes out.
4 Only by reading someone's biography // and using their product // can you understand their technological legacy.

ANSWERS

See audio script 2.06.

Speaking skill

Refer students to the *Emphasizing important information—repetition and contrastive pairs* box and ask them to read the information carefully. Explain that politicians often use techniques such as tripling in their speeches to emphasize their arguments.

1 Students listen to the clips and decide which technique is being used. Check answers as a class.

AUDIO SCRIPT 2.07

1 It wasn't the first, it wasn't the best—but it was the cheapest.

2 This is an age when we can see as many adults as children going in the same direction.

3 I ask you when this should happen. I say now, today, this minute!

4 This technology has gone. It has passed on. It has ceased to be.

5 Do you know what? I certainly know what I think, but what I am more concerned about is you.

6 So, what now? Well, all I have left to say is out with the old and in with the new.

ANSWERS

1 repetition of grammar	4 repetition of grammar
2 contrastive pairs	5 repetition of grammar
3 repetition of grammar	6 contrastive pairs

---

2 Encourage students to use topics they have encountered in the book (e.g., the decline of family meal times in the U.S., how new technology has impacted modern lifestyles, reducing car use in cities, etc.).

SPEAKING TASK

Brainstorm and plan

Ask students to brainstorm ideas with a partner. Possible qualities could include: *being innovative, experimental, brave, powerful, intelligent, persuasive, skillful*, etc.

Ask students to work individually and focus on their chosen person. Remind them of the importance of using evidence to support their arguments. Encourage them to use the mind map to help structure their ideas, and encourage them to include inversion and pausing for emphasis in their presentations. You may prefer to set this preparation stage for homework and ask students to give their speeches in the next class. Remind students that the speech should only last around three minutes, so they need to keep their arguments concise.

Speak and share

Have students practice with a partner and give each other feedback on the points listed.

Ask students to give their speeches in groups. Circulate and monitor, noting any language errors and also any good examples of inversion, stress, clear arguments, etc. to share with the class as a follow-up. If you have a small class, you may prefer each student to present to the whole class. Encourage students to listen to each other carefully and to ask questions. Use the photocopiable *Unit assignment checklist* on page 93 to assess the students' speaking.

Extra research task

Remind students of Petra, the city featured at the start of the unit that was built by the Nabataeans. Ask students to research one of the following ancient peoples (or an alternative of their choice) and the legacies they left for future generations: Incas, Ancient Greeks, Ancient Persians, Mongols, Ancient Egyptians, Romans, or Aztecs. They should prepare a short presentation for the next class giving background information and explaining their legacies.

CRITICAL THINKING SKILLS The author's position

Ask students to read the initial paragraph and the speech bubbles. Highlight the numbers in parentheses that follow each quote and refer students to the numbers in the boxes so they can see how the positions relate to the overall arguments. Ask students to read all of the contributing arguments carefully. Can they add any more? Remind students that they always need to support their overall argument with coherent contributing arguments.

Expanse

<table>
<tr><td>Critical thinking</td><td>Differentiating between fact and opinion
Identifying statements that need justification</td></tr>
<tr><td>Language development</td><td>Attitude adverbials
Abstract nouns</td></tr>
<tr><td>Pronunciation</td><td>Word stress: abstract nouns formed from adjectives</td></tr>
<tr><td>Speaking</td><td>Negotiating</td></tr>
</table>

Discussion point

Direct students' attention to the picture on page 67. Ask them if they know where it was taken (the Grand Canyon, USA). Ask what they know about the Grand Canyon and if they have been there.

Background information

The Grand Canyon is a steep canyon carved by the Colorado River. It is thought to have been created around 17 million years ago and is now considered one of the Seven Natural Wonders of the World.

Write the word *expanse* on the board. Ask students if they know what it means (a wide or open surface spread out over a large area—which could be of land or sky). Ask them how it relates to the picture (the person in the picture looks very small next to the expanse of the Grand Canyon). Then direct students' attention to the discussion questions. Allow pairs to discuss the questions, then invite students to share their ideas with the class.

Cultural awareness

Be aware that discussing salaries can be taboo in certain cultures, so students may not feel comfortable discussing this. Also note that attitudes to family size vary across cultures, e.g., the one-child policy in China has enforced the prevalence of small families. Conversely, some cultures and religions actively encourage large families (e.g., Catholic families).

Vocabulary preview

1 Ask students to complete the sentences. Mention that there is more than one possible answer in some cases. Students can check their answers in pairs before feeding back to the class.

ANSWERS

1	transcontinental	6	aloof
2	colossal/gargantuan/vast	7	proximity
3	remoteness	8	gargantuan/vast
4	extensive	9	vast
5	considerable/extensive	10	high up

2 Discuss this question as a class.

ANSWERS

The words *colossal*, *gargantuan*, and *vast* are synonyms for *enormous*.

LISTENING 1 The Trans-Siberian Railway

Before you listen

Students discuss the questions in pairs. Circulate and monitor, noting interesting comments. During feedback, ask students to share ideas with the class.

Listening

Write the word *Siberia* on the board and ask students what they know about it. Refer to the *Background information* box to provide them with more information. Play the audio and remind students to listen out for the numbers.

Background information

Siberia is a vast region of Russia and makes up 77% of Russian territory. It spreads from the Ural Mountains in the west to the Pacific Ocean. Despite its size, it only has a population of around 40 million. Little was known about life in Siberia until the Trans-Siberian Railway—which opened the region up to trade and travel. The climate in the region varies greatly. The winters are extremely cold, and the summers in the north last only one month. Most people live in the southern areas near to the railway line where the summers are warm and last for around four months.

AUDIO SCRIPT 2.08

Interviewer: The Trans-Siberian Railway is a transcontinental Russian railway network that connects hundreds of towns and cities in the European and Asian parts of Russia. Stretching out from the centre of Moscow to Vladivostok on the Sea of Japan, the 9,289-kilometre—that's approaching 6,000 miles—journey will take seven days to complete as one passes through seven time zones and two continents. It is the most extensive railroad in the world and demonstrates just how vast Russia actually is. For this week's podcast we wanted to discuss why so

shed some light on *the big(ger) picture* *breathtaking* *a vendor*
barren *hardship*

UK

many people refer to it as the special railway. With me here are two people we believe can shed some light on the topic: John Ridgeway, a freelance journalist, and Patrick Steel, a professor of Russian history. Patrick, may I start by asking you a question, which I will ask both of you; why do you consider the Trans-Siberian to be so special?

Patrick Steel: Well, considering the history of the Trans-Siberian and what the possibility of its existence meant to the Russian ruling family at the end of the nineteenth century, I would say that it has had a remarkable role to play in the development of Russia as a nation. When the Tsar Alexander III ordered the building of this great railway, he promised that it would be the soul of Russia. It was his dream to unite the country by colonizing the huge barren area from the Urals to the Pacific.

Interviewer: Wow! That was certainly a big task.

Patrick Steel: It certainly was. The Trans-Siberian winds across the most inhospitable parts of Asia, which were largely uninhabited until the early part of the twentieth century. Understandably, the remoteness of this vast land area isolated many groups of Russians across two continents, making it very difficult to rule as a nation.

Interviewer: And how did the railway make this possible?

Patrick Steel: With a continuous railroad up and running in 1914, five million people, most of them peasants, emigrated by train from European Russia to Siberia. What once used to be a ten-month journey by horse and cart was by that time possible in 72 hours by rail. Goods, services, and raw materials could be transported back and forth relatively quickly, which helped boost the economy. In terms of uniting the Russian people and increasing the proximity of Siberia to the capital, I would say that the railway has been fundamental.

Interviewer: John, you do a lot of travelling on the railway and you also mentioned the word special earlier. I think you were referring to the journey itself, weren't you?

USA

John Ridgeway: Yes, I was. From my point of view it is a special experience to travel along this railroad. And I would point to two things that for me give this journey so much romantic appeal. The first would be the Russian people you meet along the way. Russians are generally misunderstood—they have a reputation of being aloof—but to my mind when you're on a train with them, they treat you like family. You can spend up to 30 hours together with the same locals. They share any food they have with them that they think you should try—I have even been offered vegetables from a family's garden. They can really shame you with their kindness; I say that quite sincerely. I would say that the scenery may get monotonous at times, but the people do not.

Interviewer: That's really interesting. I've never actually met anyone from Russia. What was the other thing?

John Ridgeway: The very fact that you have the opportunity to cross two continents and see every part of them. Much to my delight, I have witnessed the most breathtaking landscapes. You really must make some stops along the way. I mean, you have the chance to be in the middle of Siberia! When are you ever going to have that opportunity again?

Interviewer: I'm still waiting for that chance! Now, it's also essential to understand how important the Trans-Siberian is to the people of Russia. Patrick, you mentioned this importance earlier as we were setting up the podcast …

Patrick Steel: Yes, I did. I feel that it's very difficult to speak about the railway without mentioning what it means to the people of this country. I was recently involved in a statistical study of the Trans-Siberian's significance to the country's infrastructure. To give you some examples, 80% of all goods are transported by rail; there is no transcontinental road system in Russia making it practically impossible to drive from Moscow to Vladivostok.

Interviewer: Oh, I didn't know that.

Patrick Steel: Yes, it's true. Not surprisingly, most of the quality road systems are based around Moscow and Saint Petersburg, which means that driving is only possible over short distances in other parts of the country. Furthermore, many roads in the Asian part of the country simply cannot support heavy goods vehicles, and some do not even have an asphalt surface, making rail the only option for transporting goods.

Interviewer: So, really all long-distance travelling has to be by train …

Patrick Steel: Well, a lot of Russians have to travel gargantuan distances, and that is only possible by train or plane. As flying is much more expensive and sometimes impractical depending on the destination, rail is sometimes the only option for the vast majority. Another interesting statistic we uncovered was that Russian Railways employ 1.5 million people, a considerable figure that can only be matched by the Russian army. I certainly feel that the special railway refers to the importance it has for the people.

Interviewer: John, your latest article is called "The Trans-Siberian Lifeline." Can you tell us something about that?

John Ridgeway: Yes, what happened was that the economic inactivity in the years following the collapse of the Soviet regime brought a lot of unemployment and hardship to the whole country, especially Siberia. This obliged many Siberians who had no source of earnings to turn to street vending, which in older and more prosperous times was unthinkable. Many of them became what were known as round-trip passengers on the Trans-Siberian Railway, traveling to China, Turkey, and Poland to buy cheap products to resell back home and at the stations along the route.

Interviewer: I can see now that the railroad gave them the means to travel in search of some type of income for their families.

John Ridgeway: Yes, the city of Novosibirsk became the center of such transactions as hundreds of street vendors from all over Siberia loaded with sacks of cut-price goods waited for trains to transport them hundreds of miles to their destinations and then back to their homes again. Each excursion could mean a 72-hour train ride in third-class carriages and, on average, a 12-hour wait in Novosibirsk for a train connection home.

Much to my delight *raw materials* *boost the*
surprise *peasants* *economy*
horror

Interviewer: I'm just looking at the article now, and I can see that one of the photos shows the famous housewives selling food …

John Ridgeway: Yes, these are the famous babushkas. The railway gave them the opportunity to sell homemade food at the stations—another important source of family income. As a regular traveler on the Trans-Siberian, I can tell you their tasty dishes are much better value for your money than the food served in the restaurants on the trains. So, I will echo Patrick by saying it certainly is what Russians call the railway of the people.

Interviewer: That is all we have time for, I'm afraid. Thank you both so much for coming in to speak to us today. I feel we can now understand more of the big picture and have a better idea why Russians call the Trans-Siberian a special railway.

ANSWERS

1 9289—the distance of the journey between Moscow and Vladivostok is 9289 km.
2 seven—the length of the journey between Moscow and Vladivostok is seven days
3 two—the journey passes through two continents
4 ten—it took ten months to travel from European Russia to Siberia by horse and cart
5 seventy-two—the same journey later took 72 hours by train and it was the estimated excursion time to China, Turkey, or Poland to buy goods
6 eighty—the train transports 80% of all goods
7 1.5 million—1.5 million people are employed by Russian Railways
8 twelve—the average waiting time in Novosibirsk for a connection home is 12 hours

Critical thinking skill

Ask students to read the information in the *Differentiating between fact and opinion* box. Remind them that it is important to recognize the difference between facts and opinions when they are listening to lectures or conducting their own research.

1   Give students time to read the chart and to complete the first two rows. Then play the audio and ask them to complete the chart. They can then check their answers in pairs before feeding back to the class.

AUDIO SCRIPT   2.09

The Trans-Siberian Railway—Extract one
Interviewer: The Trans-Siberian Railway is a transcontinental Russian railway network that connects hundreds of towns and cities in the European and Asian parts of Russia. Stretching out from the centre of Moscow to Vladivostok on the Sea of Japan, the 9,289-kilometre—that's approaching 6,000 miles—journey will take seven days to complete as one passes through seven time zones

and two continents. It is the most extensive railroad in the world and demonstrates just how vast Russia actually is.

The Trans-Siberian Railway—Extract two
John Ridgeway: Yes, I was. From my point of view it is a special experience to travel along this railroad. And I would point to two things that for me give this journey so much romantic appeal. The first would be the Russian people you meet along the way. Russians are generally misunderstood—they have a reputation of being aloof—but to my mind when you're on a train with them, they treat you like family. You can spend up to 30 hours together with the same locals. They share any food they have with them that they think you should try—I have even been offered vegetables from a family's garden. They can really shame you with their kindness; I say that quite sincerely. I would say that the scenery may get monotonous at times, but the people do not.

POSSIBLE ANSWERS

	Statement 1: Russia is a huge country.	Statement 2: Russian people are friendly and interesting.
Do you have any experience or knowledge of the topic?	Answers will vary. Answer will be yes for most students.	Answers will vary.
Does the statement fit with your experience or knowledge?	Possible answer: Yes, I know Russia is the biggest country in the world.	Answers will vary.
Is there any language to signal opinion?	No	*to my mind*
What evidence is presented (if any)?	The railway line that crosses it is 9,289 km. (and passes through seven time zones and two continents).	Russian people on the train treated the speaker like family and offered him food.
Does the evidence prove the statement? Why or why not?	Yes. 9,289 km. is measurable and can be compared against measurements of other countries.	Possible answer: No. This is just one person's experience of a very small proportion of the Russian population.
Is it fact or opinion?	Fact	Opinion

a pursuit   to compel   a crest   with a single goal
compelling   to scale   an incentive

2 Ask the students to do this exercise individually.

ANSWERS
1 F	2 O	3 F	4 F	5 F	6 O

3 Play the audio again, then allow time for students to compare their answers with a partner before feeding back to the class.

Developing critical thinking

While groups discuss the questions, circulate and make a note of any interesting comments. Invite students to share their ideas with the class as a follow-up. Encourage them to give reasons for their opinions.

EXTENSION ACTIVITY

Ask students to research one of the following small and densely populated countries online: Bangladesh, Bahrain, Singapore, or Barbados. They should also research one of the following sparsely populated countries: Iceland, Australia, Mongolia, or Mauritania.

They should look for the following information: exact population, size of country, transportation, standard of living (GDP), economy, cost of accommodation.

Ask them to prepare a short presentation including a fact file on their two countries, followed by a decision on where they would prefer to live and why. Ensure that students know they need to justify their choices.

LISTENING 2 Why do people climb mountains?

Before you listen

1 Check that students can pronounce the adjectives correctly by drilling the words with the class. Pairs can then choose their adjectives. Check that they understand the meanings of the adjectives.

2 Invite pairs to tell the class which adjectives they selected and why.

3 Ask students to explain their choices to the class.

Listening

Tell students to check the adjectives that are connected with what the speaker says. Play the audio. Students can then check their answers in pairs before feeding back to the class. *American accent*

AUDIO SCRIPT 2.10

Before his fatal mission to climb the colossal Mount Everest in 1924, renowned mountaineer George Leigh Mallory was asked why he wanted to climb it. To this question he gave a short and simple answer: "Because it is there." Mallory and his climbing partner disappeared when they

---

were only a few hundred meters from the summit. His fate remained unknown until his frozen body was discovered 75 years later. His rather dismissive response to that final question was actually hiding the whole truth of the matter. Why do we climb mountains? The obvious answer would be to say, "To get to the top." However, I would say that is simply not the case. It is understandably exciting to reach the summit, but this is only an end. It does not take into consideration the means. Many individuals are mystified about why someone would risk their life going up and down a mountain, and then have nothing to show as a result. However, it is not the result that we should be focusing on.

You may even suggest that it is the risk involved in the climb. I must say that many climbers admit that they enjoy the adrenalin rush as they face danger. But, once again, I would call that an oversimplification. Mountain climbing is problematic, hazardous, and often painful. So why do people do it? People climb mountains because they love the pursuit itself. The means to this enjoyment consists of many factors.

First of all, mountaineering brings a group of people together with a single goal. The group acts as one, and you have to understand your fellow climbers and the situation you are in. Cooperation is needed to succeed, and unity must prevail.

Then there is the challenge. Scaling a steep slope is a trial to be overcome very much like the trials of life. If you see a barrier, you can't pretend it isn't there; you have to get over it or under it. Our next step could be deadly, but it could equally be rewarding. Climbing allows us to create our own reward sequence, a source of satisfaction we can go back to again and again. An uphill slope represents an incentive, and a peak symbolizes achievement. Naturally, climbing also compels us to explore and extend our physical limitations. It also lets us study the interactions between our minds and our bodies. This is a pursuit that allows us to really get to know ourselves and what we are capable of.

Let's not overlook the fact that it also allows us to see the splendor of nature. Imagine the beauty of being high up on a mountain peak when the sun begins to rise and being the first one to see it. There is no greater artist than Mother Nature herself, and there is no better place to appreciate this than from high above on a mountain crest.

Oddly enough, there is also another side to climbing a mountain that many people would not think of, and that is creativity. As we make our ascent, we feel like artists creating our own work of art. Making a new route that has never been trodden before gives us the same feeling of originality. Eventually, climbing becomes part of us, and we feel we need to do it. Why do artists paint the pictures they do? They do it because they need to. This possibly explains Mallory's response to that famous question in 1924—"Because it is there."

ANSWER
All adjectives correspond except *exhausting*.

renowned   fate   mystified   the adrenalin rush
an oversimplification

Critical thinking skill

Ask students to read the information in the *Identifying statements that need justification* box. Highlight the importance of recognizing statements that need justification when they take notes in lectures.

1 Ask students to work individually to check the statements that require justification.

ANSWERS
Statements 1, 2, 4, and 6 require justification.

2 Play the audio again and ask students to note down the justifications given.

ANSWERS
1
Justification—One of the factors of enjoyment is cooperation.
2
Justification—(Both life and climbing) have barriers that have to be overcome.
4
Justification—It compels us to explore and extend our physical limitations.
6
Justification—We feel like artists and have the same feeling of originality when we create a new route.

3 Ask students to compare their answers with a partner.

Developing critical thinking

1 Allow time for groups to discuss the questions. Other activities could include marathon running, sky diving, trekking through a jungle, etc.

2 Ask students to think back to both listening texts in the unit. Remind them that both are connected with size and expanse. Then ask groups to discuss the questions. Circulate and note any interesting comments. Invite students to share their ideas with the class.

Language development: Attitude adverbials

Ask students to read the information in the *Attitude adverbials* box. Highlight that these adverbials are useful in spoken English, but should be avoided in written academic English.

1 Ask students to work individually to insert the adverbials and then check answers as a class.

2 Ask students to write their sentences individually.

3 Have students compare their sentences with a partner. During feedback, invite individual students to write their sentences on the board for analysis.

POSSIBLE ANSWERS
Note: The adverbs can all go in the three positions as mentioned in the box, except for 3 and 5, in which *personally* and *ideally* can either come before or after the subject, though *ideally* would commonly come before the subject.
1 **Not surprisingly**, most of the quality road systems are based around Moscow and Saint Petersburg.
2 **Understandably**, the remoteness of this vast land area isolated many groups of Russians across two continents, making it very difficult to rule as a nation.
3 I **personally** believe the Russians are friendly people.
4 Climbing is **undoubtedly** a dangerous pursuit.
5 **Ideally**, you should go climbing with a team.
6 **Honestly**, I have never seen anything as beautiful as a sunrise from the top of a mountain crest.

Language development: Abstract nouns

Ask students to read the information in the *Abstract nouns* box. Remind students that understanding how to create word families with suffixes can really help them to expand their vocabulary.

1 Ask students to work individually to complete the extracts. They can then check their answers in pairs before feeding back to the class.

ANSWERS
1 possibility; existence; development
2 kindness
3 importance
4 inactivity; unemployment; hardship
5 unity
6 satisfaction
7 achievement

2 Ask students to put the words from exercise 1 in the correct column.

ANSWERS
-ment: develop, employ, acheive	-ence: exist
	-ance: important
-action: satisfy	-ship: hard
-y: unite	-ity: possible, active
-ness: kind	

3 Have students complete the sentences with nouns from exercise 1. Check answers as a class.

ANSWERS
1 inactivity	4 existence
2 unemployment	5 achievement
3 satisfaction	6 development

EXTENSION ACTIVITY

Write the following words on the board: *related* (adj), *selfish* (adj), *stable* (adj), *violent* (adj), *attractive* (adj), *attain* (v), *dominate* (v). Ask students to identify the word types.

Drill the words to check that students can pronounce them using the correct stress (see underlining). Then ask students to work in pairs to formulate the nouns for each word and any other members of the word family they can think of. They can use their dictionaries if they need help.

Ask students to share their answers with the class. Write their suggestions on the board and encourage students to identify the stressed syllables.

Answers: re*la*tion, re*la*tionship, re*late*; *self*ishness; sta*bil*ity, *stab*ilize, stabili*za*tion; *vio*lence, *vio*late; attra*ctive*ness, attra*ction*, attr*act*; att*ain*ment; domi*na*tion, *dom*inant, domi*neer*ing.

Ask students to work individually to write seven sentences using the nouns they have formed. They can compare answers in pairs before feeding back to the class. Invite students to write their sentences on the board and to read them aloud so you can check their use of word stress.

SPEAKING Organizing a cultural program

Pronunciation skill

Ask students to read the information in the *Word stress: abstract nouns formed from adjectives* box. Remind students that word stress often changes within word families.

1   Ask students to underline the stressed syllables.

ANSWERS

See the underlined syllables in audio script 2.11.

2   Play the audio so that students can check their answers. Check answers with the class and drill the words to ensure students are confident with the word stress.

AUDIO SCRIPT 2.11

1 pos*sible*	possi*bil*ity
2 *sat*isfy	satis*fac*tion
3 ex*ist*	ex*ist*ence
4 a*chieve*	a*chieve*ment
5 de*vel*op	de*vel*opment
6 im*por*tant	im*por*tance
7 in*ac*tive	ina*ctiv*ity
8 em*ploy*	em*ploy*ment

ANSWERS

-ity and *-tion* endings cause a change in stress.
With nouns ending in *-ity*, the stress moves to the syllable before *-ity*.
With nouns ending in *-ion*, the stress moves to the second to last syllable.

Speaking skill

Ask students to read the information in the *Negotiating* box. Remind them that they will often be asked to collaborate with other students in project work and for presentations, so negotiating language will be extremely useful to them.

1   Play the audio and ask students to check any language in the box that they hear. They should also note what decision the speakers made.

AUDIO SCRIPT   2.12

A: OK, I'd like to suggest that we begin by looking at the practical applications of Larsson's theory. Are you happy with that?

B: Uh, that would be good, but I think perhaps we need to clarify what exactly the theory is saying, first of all. What do you think about that?

A: I'm not sure it's really necessary. I mean, I think everyone listening to our presentation will already be pretty familiar with the theory. I think we should just get straight to the main point. B: But there have been different interpretations of the theory, and I think it would be helpful to make it clear how we've interpreted it, before we go any further. What would be wrong with doing that?

A: Well, it's just that we only have 20 minutes for the presentation, and I don't think there will be enough time to cover the other points we want to make.

B: OK, I see your point. Perhaps we could just include a very brief clarification …

A: Agreed. So, we'll start by saying—quickly—how we interpret the theory, and then we'll look at its practical applications. Next, …

ANSWERS

Expressions used in the discussion:
I'd like to suggest that
Are you happy with that?
I think perhaps
What do you think about that?
I think we should
What would be wrong with doing that?
Perhaps we could
They decide to include a brief clarification of the theory.

2   Students work with a partner. Remind them to use language from the *Negotiating* box during their negotiations.

This is a good place to use the video resource *Infinite boundaries*. It is located in the Video resources section of the digital component.

SPEAKING TASK

Brainstorm and plan

Ask students to work in groups for the *Brainstorm* stage. If your students are not overly familiar with their university's city, they may need access to the Internet during this stage to help them find places to visit.

Subdivide the groups so that students now work in pairs. Encourage them to write down their program.

Speak and share

Put students into new pairs so they are talking to someone from a different group. Refer them to the language on page 74 and encourage them to use these phrases during their negotiation. Monitor their use of negotiating language. Ensure
that they come to an agreement and finalize their programs.

Put students back into their original pairs so that they can share their new programs. Make sure they justify their statements when they explain their decisions. Circulate and note good use of language. Give feedback, writing good examples of language on the board as well as any language that needs correcting. Use the photocopiable *Unit assignment checklist* on page 94 to assess the students' speaking.

Extra research task

Tell students to plan a year of traveling with a friend. Ask them to research the countries online they would like to go to and what they would like to see there. They should note their plan for the year, including how they will travel, where they will go and why, what they will see in those places and why, and how long they will stay in each location. Ask them to bring the plans to the next lesson, then have them work in pairs to compare their plans and to negotiate a travel plan to do together.

STUDY SKILLS Organizing your personal study online

Getting started

Ask students to discuss the questions in pairs. Encourage them to give reasons for their answers.

Scenario

Ask students to read about Haru and make a note of advice they would give him. Students can compare their suggestions with a partner. During class feedback, write any useful tips on the board.

POSSIBLE ANSWER
Haru could develop better self-study strategies to organize his time more effectively. He needs to schedule his week so that he has time available for research. He needs to learn how to use academic search engines. He needs more self-discipline not to get distracted by other Internet media while online. He also needs to find a suitable space for studying. This might mean negotiating with the other people in his house to give him quiet time or finding an empty classroom to use.

Consider it

Write the word *procrastinate* on the board and ask students if they know what it means (to delay or postpone action). Give an example of how this can affect students in their studies, e.g., you have an essay to write, but you decide to tidy your bedroom first, or you spend days researching but make no progress. Allow time for students to read through the tips and to note which ones they have tried. Ask students to share their experiences with the class.

Over to you

Students work with a partner. Encourage them to give reasons and examples. Then invite students to share their ideas with the class and write any useful tips on the board.

Critical thinking	Maximizing language Recognizing implicit assumptions
Language development	Expressing change Gradeable adjectives
Pronunciation	Intonation and tonic prominence
Speaking	Adding points to an argument

Discussion point

Direct students' attention to the picture on page 77. Ask them what they can see (a caterpillar changing into a chrysalis, which will then go on to change into a butterfly). Ask them how the picture is connected to the unit heading, *Change* (it's an example of how dramatic change occurs in nature and that change is an inevitable part of life, so it is important to be able to adapt to change).

Students can now discuss the questions with a partner. Circulate and note any interesting comments. Invite students to share their ideas with the class.

EXTENSION ACTIVITY

Brainstorm as a class any major changes that can occur in someone's life and write suggestions on the board (e.g., moving house/city/country, new government coming into power in your country, getting married, a new job / losing your job, family break-up / divorce). Ask students to work with a partner to brainstorm some tips on how to cope well with change. Pairs should then share their ideas with the class. Write their suggestions on the board. Ideas could include the following:

- See change as an opportunity.
- Try not to complain or blame others when a change is difficult.
- Notice the signs of when change may occur and prepare for it.
- Accept that change is part of life and cannot be avoided.

Vocabulary preview

1 Ask students to work individually to do the exercise. They can then check their answers in pairs before feeding back to the class.

ANSWERS
1 frequently	6 it is expected to live
2 comes out of an egg	7 buying or selling something
3 under the ground	
4 has offspring	8 problem with no apparent solution
5 outside its body	

2 Discuss this question as a whole class.

ANSWER
fluctuates

LISTENING 1 Metamorphosis—the secrets behind nature's amazing change

Before you listen

Refer students to the definition of metamorphosis in the box, then ask them to fill in the table. Remind them of the picture on page 77, which is an example of metamorphosis. Students can then compare their ideas with a partner before feeding back to the class. Then ask students to look at the words in the *Academic keywords* box. Check that they are clear on the meanings and that they can pronounce the words correctly. They can refer to their dictionaries if they need help.

Listening

Ask students to look at the pictures of the cicada. Do they know anything about this creature? They will learn more about it in the audio. Students should read the numbers and the notes, checking that they understand the vocabulary (they may need help with *nymphs* = the immature form of an insect, *molting* = shedding a coat or outer covering, *decibel* = a unit that measures the intensity/volume of sound). Then play the audio while students complete the notes on page 79. They can then check their answers in pairs before feeding back to the class.

Background information

The audio describes the lifecycle of the periodical cicada, which is native to eastern North America. It has been studied extensively, partly due to the fact that it matures every 13 or 17 years. Mathematicians have shown interest in the fact that the prime numbers 13 and 17 are involved, and have sought to discover why. The theory is that the periodical cicada has evolved to avoid the lifecycles of their own predators. Most lifecycles are divisible by two or by five, but the numbers 13 and 17 are not. This helps the cicada, e.g., if the cicada has a life cycle of 17 years and its predator has a life cycle of five years, then they will only meet every (17 x 5) = 85 years, which is the least common multiple of the two numbers.

AUDIO SCRIPT 2.13

Professor: After biding their time underground for 17 years, these creatures rise from the ground and march like zombies to the nearest tree. Starting to climb, they begin their final journey to unleash millions of their kind into just a few acres of land.

Well, good morning, everyone. I hope that has woken you all up and you are intrigued. ...

As you know, this is the final lecture on metamorphosis, and our final topic is the periodical cicada. The cicada is a flying, plant-feeding insect found in most parts of the world. There are two main types: the annual cicada, which appears every year and the periodical cicada, which only appears every 13 or 17 years, depending on the species.

It's the remarkable life cycle of the periodical cicada that we will look at today in order to consider a conundrum that has puzzled experts for decades. Why do they wait so long to complete their metamorphosis? And why do they all appear at the same time? Let's start by looking at the 17-year variety's peculiar life cycle.

Newly born cicada nymphs burrow into the ground to feed from liquid around plant roots. For the next 17 years, they go through five stages of molting—that is, losing their old skin—and growing as they move deeper and deeper into the ground. When they finally emerge almost two decades later, they climb the nearest tree to molt one final time. Then they spend six days waiting for their exoskeleton to harden before they embark on the final three weeks of their lives. Their short life above ground has one purpose: reproduction.

To begin with, the males sing a species-specific mating song to attract the females. In North America, three different species of cicada appear at the same time, each with its specific mating call. Most of the mating happens in these "chorus trees." Remember, millions of these insects emerge in the same small area of land, that, as you can imagine, will create considerable noise pollution for people living nearby. The mass singing can reach 100 decibels and can be heard from up to one and a half kilometers away. That's equivalent to someone using a chainsaw six meters away from you.

With mating finally over, the females lay approximately 20 eggs in the branches of young trees. The eggs then hatch, and the newly born nymphs drop to the ground to begin the 17-year cycle all over again. // stop + check

This brings us to our scientific conundrum. Periodical cicadas crawl out of their subterranean hideouts every 13 or 17 years. This fact has raised considerable interest with mathematicians. Why? Well, 13 and 17 are prime numbers. These are numbers only divisible by themselves and 1. The big question is whether the emergences of periodical cicada are timed to prime numbers by coincidence or is there some deeper mechanism behind it?

Paleontologist Stephen Jay Gould believed that the prime number life cycle is no coincidence. He said that it actually evolved as an effort to avoid predators. Many species evolve in different ways to protect themselves against attackers: they can grow spines or thick shells, and they can even taste bad or be poisonous. The periodical cicada appears to have developed its own time period defense system. Many predators have two- to five-year life cycles. If the cicadas appeared every two or five years, their life cycle would coincide with those of their predators.

By springing forth in their millions every 13 or 17 years, periodical cicadas not only minimize the chance of predators eating them all at once, but they also maximize their chances of avoiding appearing during the predator's average lifetime.

Glen Webb, a mathematician at Vanderbilt University, sought to prove the life-cycle theory by setting up a series of experiments in which mathematical models of the emergence of periodical cicadas were compared with those of imaginary predators with two- and three-year life cycles. His results prove that Gould's argument could indeed be a valid one as no predator coincided with the cicada.

However, this has also been disputed, as many scientists say that it was not predators but climate that shaped the periodical cicada's life cycle. The cicada is believed to have evolved at the end of the last ice age, a time when glaciers advanced and retreated across North America.

Doctors C. E. Carlton and R. T. Cox have proposed a theory that, during this time, cicada reproduction often failed as summer temperatures failed to reach the 68 degrees required to support the insect's life during the four critical weeks of flight and mating. The cicadas with a longer life cycle—those that spent more time underground—had a greater chance of avoiding cool summers and therefore reproduced in greater numbers than their cousins with shorter life cycles. They eventually became dominant in the gene pool, while the others died out.

Yet, that doesn't explain why the cicadas settled on a 13- and 17-year cycle, and not 11, 19, or some other prime number. One thing we can be sure of, though, is that the periodical cicada has evolved over time to ensure its own survival.

ANSWERS

1 13 or 17	3 3	5 1.5	7 68
2 5	4 100	6 20	

Critical thinking skill

Ask students to read the information in the *Maximizing language* box. Remind them that maximizing language helps speakers to show their audience how important they believe a topic to be.

1 Ask students to read the text carefully, then play the audio to allow them to write down the differences. You may need to pause the audio in the various places to allow time for students to note down the actual language used. Ask students to compare their answers in pairs to help them fill in any gaps. Then check answers with the class.

AUDIO SCRIPT 2.14

Professor: After biding their time underground for 17 years, these creatures rise from the ground and march like zombies to the nearest tree. Starting to climb, they begin their final journey to unleash millions of their kind into just a few acres of land.

Well, good morning everyone. I hope that has woken you all up and you are intrigued.

As you know, this is the final lecture on metamorphosis, and our final topic is the periodical cicada. The cicada is a flying, plant-feeding insect found in most parts of the world. There are two main types: the annual cicada, which appears every year and the periodical cicada, which only appears every 13 or 17 years, depending on the species.

It's the remarkable life cycle of the periodical cicada that we will look at today in order to consider a conundrum that has puzzled experts for decades. Why do they wait so long to complete their metamorphosis? And why do they all appear at the same time? Let's start by looking at the 17-year variety's peculiar life cycle.

POSSIBLE ANSWERS

Student annotation may vary. The actual audio script is: After **biding their time** underground for 17 years, these **creatures rise from** the ground and **march like zombies** to the nearest tree. **Starting to climb, they begin their final journey to unleash millions** of their kind into **just** a few acres of land. … **It's the remarkable life cycle of the periodical cicada** that we will look at today in order to consider **a conundrum** that has puzzled experts **for decades**. Why do they wait so long to complete their metamorphosis? And why do they all **appear** at the same time? Let's start by looking at the 17-year variety's **peculiar** life cycle.

2 Discuss the questions as a whole class.

ANSWERS

For the maximized language, see the words in bold in the answer key for exercise 1. The speaker wants to convey the sense of scale of this phenomenon.

EXTENSION ACTIVITY

Tell students to write down ten adjectives with a partner. Once they have done this, they should give their list to another pair. This pair should put the ten adjectives into sentences. They don't have to write ten sentences; they can have more than one adjective in each sentence. Once they have done that, they should pass their ten sentences to another pair. This time students should adapt the sentences by using maximizing language to give them more impact. After they have done this, elicit one or two sentences from each pair.

Developing critical thinking

Before they begin their discussions, brainstorm some interesting naturally occurring processes and write them on the board (e.g., *erupting volcano, locust storm, earthquake, cliff erosion, trees losing their leaves*, etc.). Students discuss the questions in small groups. Circulate and make a note of any interesting comments. Invite students to share their experiences with the class.

LISTENING 2 A global tax on changing money?

Before you listen

1 Ask students to discuss the questions with a partner. If they have access to the Internet in class, ask them to find out the exact exchange rates for their currencies. Invite students to share their answers with the class.

2 Ask students what they can see in the picture (city traders). Ask if any of them would like a job as a city trader, and why or why not. Now ask them to complete the information individually. They can check their answers in pairs before feeding back to the class. Then have them discuss the questions.

ANSWERS

1 lending	3 risky
2 speculation	4 profit

Listening

Ask students to look at the *Academic keywords* box at the bottom of the page. Check they understand the meanings and that they can pronounce the words correctly. Explain that they will hear these words being used in the audio. Now ask students to read the questions and the multiple choice options. Provide help with vocabulary if necessary. Then play the audio so that students can choose the correct answers. Check answers with the whole class.

Exam tip

In the IELTS Test, the third listening section is a dialogue between two speakers. The multiple choice question type given in this task is also common in the IELTS Test. If you have students preparing for the IELTS Test, you could explain this and point out that a useful strategy is to underline key words in each option and to think of synonyms before they listen.

all women again

AUDIO SCRIPT 2.15

Announcer: Hello, and welcome back to Money Talks. And let me begin with a question. Have you ever changed money before, when travelling abroad, for example? Do you know the value of your national currency? Does the exchange rate change a lot? Today we're discussing changing money and an interesting proposal for the world's economy. We are joined by two economists, Mrs. Sue Mawer and Dr. Barbara Jenkins.

Mrs. Mawer & Dr. Jenkins: Hello.

Announcer: Now, Mrs. Mawer. Why don't you explain the idea of a currency tax?

Mrs. Mawer: Thank you. The idea isn't a new one. It goes back more than 30 years. Specifically to 1978. In this year James Tobin, a Nobel Prize winner for economics, first presented his plan for a tax on currency transactions. The tax was intended to discourage the speculations that are blamed for large exchange rate fluctuations and serious damage to national economies.

Announcer: What do you mean, speculations?

Mrs. Mawer: Well, what you need to understand is that more than one and a half trillion dollars is exchanged every day on the global money markets. Of this huge amount of money, more than 80% of this trading is buying and selling money to make a profit. This is also called speculation. Financiers buy money in one currency and then trade it quickly into another to make a profit. That's fine, but this speculation has played a very important role in the financial crises that have rocked the world's economy over the past 20 years. As speculators have bought and sold currency, they have affected its value. And that value has an impact in terms of trade. If suddenly your currency is in demand, and value goes up, then the cost of your goods to other countries goes up, too. That can have a massive impact on consumer goods, agriculture, and ultimately, on the money in people's pockets.

Announcer: So you think a currency tax is a good idea. Explain why.

Mrs. Mawer: Well, Tobin's plan was to slightly increase the cost of trading in currencies, by introducing the currency transactions tax—costing the banks and other institutions more money to get involved in this kind of trade. I think this minimal tax is a good idea, as it would help slow down this kind of speculation. Currencies would change value less frequently, and there would be more stability.

Announcer: Dr. Jenkins, you disagree. Why?

Dr. Jenkins: Mrs. Mawer is right that there is speculation in the money markets, and this can be harmful to the world economy. But a tax on money exchanges won't improve anything. In fact, it would do the opposite and hurt the economy. If we put more tax on trading, either for money trading or any other kind of trading, it will slow down an economy. This will hurt especially the weaker economies.

Announcer: There is another question though, isn't there? What would we do with all this tax income if we did introduce the tax?

Mrs. Mawer: The small tax that is being suggested would be used to help poorer countries. Even if we introduced a 0.1% tax on exchanges, we could raise between 50 and 300 billion dollars. The United Nations estimates that with

225 billion dollars world poverty could be eliminated. Currently they spend around ten million per year.

Dr. Jenkins: Again, I think this is just wishful thinking. What Mrs. Mawer suggests sounds very noble, but the truth is that countries that receive huge amounts of financial aid become accustomed to relying on that income. What we need is for those countries to create and develop their own efficient economy.

Mrs. Mawer: I don't think that is the case ...

Dr. Jenkins: And how can we assume that the rich countries, who are likely to be the ones collecting this revenue, will share the money with their less well-off neighbours? It's quite possible that they would want to keep it themselves.

Mrs. Mawer: You could easily set up international laws to determine where the money is distributed.

Dr. Jenkins: Yes, but who would enforce those laws? How would you guarantee fair distribution?

Announcer: It looks like we have two very different points of view here.

Dr. Jenkins: Well, Mrs. Mawer seems to assume that collecting this tax will be easy. But who is going to do it? What happens when people avoid the tax, or begin to move money around illegally? It's an impossible situation to police in this globalised world.

Mrs. Mawer: Well, tax evasion should not be an excuse for not introducing a tax. If the argument is we should not have a law because people can break it, then the whole idea of justice is pointless. The fact of the matter is that a very small tax on so many transactions could make a big difference in the world.

Dr. Jenkins: Yes, we all want to see a better and fairer world. But I can't quite see how this measure would accomplish that. I personally think it would make things worse.

ANSWERS
1 b   2 b   3 a   4 b   5 b

Critical thinking skill

Refer students to the *Recognizing implicit assumptions* box and ask them to read it carefully. Highlight the fact that recognizing implicit assumptions is another tool for ensuring that students think critically about what they read, rather than just accepting what other people have written about a topic. This is an integral part of being a good university student.

1   Ask students to read the three extracts. Play the audio so they can complete the extracts. Students can check their answers in pairs before feeding back to the class. It may be necessary to refer to the audio script to help students see the implicit assumptions in context and understand them fully.

ANSWERS
1 goes up; massive impact; people's pockets
2 put more; slow down; hurt
3 huge amounts; relying on; create and develop

2 Ask students to circle the correct option for each extract.

> **ANSWERS**
> 1 negative   **3** a bad thing
> 2 discourages

Developing critical thinking

1 Ask students to discuss the questions in small groups. Circulate and monitor, noting any interesting comments. Invite students to share their ideas with the class.

2 Ask students what they can remember about *Listening 1*. Write a few of their recollections on the board. Now ask students to think about both of the listening texts. They can then discuss the questions. Again, circulate and note any interesting information. Also make a note of any language problems for correction after the discussion task. Write any incorrect sentences on the board for peer correction, taking care to change a few words so as not to single out individual students.

Language development: Expressing change

Ask students to read the information in the *Expressing change* box. Check that students understand the difference between transitive and intransitive verbs (verbs with or without objects). Ask students to look up the five different verbs in their dictionaries and to make a note of their slight differences in meaning. Make sure students record any dependent prepositions and verb patterns which change the meaning of the verbs, e.g., *adapt to, adapt for, adapt something for something.*

1 Remind students that when they express an opinion in a seminar/tutorial, it is good to use a variety of vocabulary as it will help them to be clear and specific. Now ask students to read the six sentences with the verb *change* and to decide which synonyms to use for each. Students can check answers in pairs before feeding back to the class.

> **POSSIBLE ANSWERS**
> 1 adapted/adjusted   **4** transform
> 2 convert   **5** adjust
> 3 vary   **6** converted

2 Ask students to work with a partner to find more verbs, using a thesaurus if they choose to. They should then check the exact meanings in a dictionary. Ask students to note down meanings and collocations when they find them. If students are struggling to think of additional verbs, remind them that they looked at ways of expressing change in Unit 5 (page 53). They could look back at this page

to refresh their memories, and they may find some other verbs. Once they have researched their three new verbs thoroughly, ask them to answer the two questions about those verbs. Ask individual students to share their findings with the class as a follow-up.

> **POSSIBLE ANSWERS**
> shift, develop, evolve, modify, alter, turn into, revise

3 Have students work with a partner to ask and answer the questions. They should take turns to be the person who asks. Circulate and note any interesting comments. Invite students to share their ideas with the class and make sure they use the verbs connected to change where possible.

This is a good place to use the video resource *Shock to the system*. It is located in the Video resources section of the digital component. Alternatively, remind students about the video so they can do this at home.

Language development: Gradeable adjectives

Ask students to read the information in the *Gradeable adjectives* box and check that they understand it.

1 Remind students that they need to make decisions about the adjectives in bold—are they gradeable or non-gradeable? Students may know instinctively which kind of adjective they are, or they may need to rely on meaning to help them decide. Students can then check their answers in pairs before feeding back to the class.

> **ANSWERS**
> 1 very   **4** a little
> 2 a little   **5** a little
> 3 practically

2 Highlight that there is only one mistake in each extract, so students need to read them carefully to decide where the mistake lies. They can then check their answers in pairs before feeding back to the class.

> **ANSWERS**
> **1**
> Not only is technology a forum for sharing and presenting existing knowledge, it also provides a ~~very~~ unique opportunity to create new knowledge. This creates superior knowledge.
> **2**
> There is an absolutely infinite choice of learning tools using technology, it's true. But it's also true that a ~~quite~~ huge choice of possible distractions exist. Social media, instant messaging, and online games can detract from learning.
> **3**
> Face-to-face learning is ~~virtually~~ important for many reasons, such as group work and real-world

application of tasks. It's almost impossible to reproduce these conditions online.

4

Businesses and commercial interests are mainly responsible for many technological changes in the classroom. Teachers and students play a ~~very~~ miniscule part in these changes.

SPEAKING Holding a debate about educational changes

Pronunciation skill

Ask students to read the information in the *Intonation and tonic prominence* box. Highlight that there are three aspects to tonic prominence (volume, speed, and tone). Remind them that recognizing this prominence can help them identify key facts in lectures, and being able to replicate this skill will enhance their fluency in English.

Ask students to read the sentences, then play the audio so that they can underline the tonic prominence in each response. You may need to play the audio twice to allow students enough time to make their decisions. They can then compare their answers with a partner before feeding back to the class.

AUDIO SCRIPT 2.16

1
A: I didn't understand what the professor was talking about.
B: I had no idea what the professor was talking about.
2
A: Can you lend me your notes on the first lecture?
B: I didn't take any notes on the first lecture.
3
A: We don't know if this tax will work.
B: I don't think anybody knows if this tax will work.
4
A: You could set up laws to decide where the money goes.
B: Yes, but who would enforce those laws to decide where the money goes?

ANSWERS
1 B: I had <u>no</u> idea what the professor was talking about.
2 B: I didn't take <u>any</u> notes on the first lecture.
3 B: I don't think <u>anybody</u> knows if this tax will work.
4 B: Yes, but who would <u>enforce</u> those laws to decide where the money goes?

Speaking skill

Ask students to read the information in the *Adding points to an argument* box. Remind them that these signaling words and phrases are formal, so they are useful when they are giving academic presentations or speaking in seminars, but would occur less frequently in informal spoken English.

Students should then underline the signaling words and phrases, and number the sentences. They should check their answers with a partner. Ask students to decide which syllables should be stressed and to practice reading the paragraph aloud to their partner. Circulate and monitor, noting use of intonation. Ask a strong student to model the intonation for the whole class.

ANSWERS
a Moreover; 5
b I would like to argue; 1
c more than sufficient; 3
d My main reason; 2
e What is more; 4

Speaking Task

Brainstorm and plan

Write the words *digital* and *analog* on the board. Ask them which means there is a physical presence of something that you can touch and see (*analog*). Then, ask students to work with a partner to brainstorm more assumptions for each heading in the table. When they have finished, ask students to share their ideas with the class. Write their suggestions on the board.

Background information

Their ideas could include the following (add these to the board if they have not been mentioned):

New generation is digital

Digital technology is central to the modern workplace and increasingly the home.

Smartphone and tablet usage is extremely high among young people.

Social networking and connecting with others online is popular amongst young people.

Some educational organizations are using MOOC's (Massive Online Open Courses) to respond to the ways in which the younger generation likes to learn.

Education is analog and needs to change

Students are taught by teachers, not by computers.

Many exams are written by hand, not on the computer.

Marking and assessment needs a teacher and generally is not done digitally.

Books and worksheets are often used, rather than interactive whiteboards, etc.

Divide the class into three groups. Groups 1 and 2 should refer back to the language points on pages 79 and 84 during their preparation. Group 3 needs to add more evaluation points to their checklist. If they are struggling, they should look back through the unit at the language and skills that have been covered.

Speak and share

The students now hold the debate. Remind them to take notes when others are speaking (this should include those in group 3). After each group has presented their arguments, allow time for students to come up with counter-arguments. During this time, group 3 can fill in their evaluation charts. Then restart the discussion so that students can present the counter arguments. (Group 3 can add to or change their evaluation forms during this phase.)

Allow a few minutes for group 3 to decide which group made the best argument. They should then provide feedback to both groups, giving reasons for their evaluation. During this stage, monitor and take language notes. Use the photocopiable *Unit assignment checklist* on page 95 to assess the students' speaking.

Extra research task

Write the following statement on the board:

Technology can never replace the teacher in language learning. It can only be a tool, not a tutor.

Ask students to conduct online research to find out what has been written about this topic. They should find two or three sources. Ask them to make notes on what they read and to ensure they also note down the source. Then ask them to make up their own mind about the statement. In the next class, students can share their findings and discuss their opinions on the statement.

Exam tip

Although this section has been a spoken debate, this type of question is quite similar to an IELTS part 2 writing task. Students commonly have to look at different sides of a debate and write about these different perspectives. As an extension to the discussion, you could ask students to imagine their discussion was a brainstorm for an essay on the topic. Tell students to choose three of the main points raised in their debate and put them into an essay plan. They should then compare their essay plans in groups of three.

CRITICAL THINKING SKILLS Argument and disagreement

Write the words *disagreement* and *argument* on the board. Ask students to think about these words in an academic context and to describe the difference between them. Don't give any answers at this point—ask them to read the first paragraph and the key terms on the page.

You may need to check their understanding. Explain the following: the aim in the academic world is to present sound arguments, not simply to disagree with others. This means that giving reasons and evidence is absolutely imperative, and the ultimate goal for students should be to persuade others to agree with their way of thinking by using arguments backed up with evidence.

Now ask students to read the rest of the page. Be prepared to clarify any points if necessary.

UNIT 9 FLOW

Critical thinking	Identifying counter-arguments Visual aids and diagrams
Language development	Irregular plurals Words in context—working with concordance data
Pronunciation	Intonation to express hesitation and doubt
Speaking	Softening criticism

ANSWERS

1	aquatic	6	contamination
2	Evaporation	7	compelling
3	contemplating	8	Intrinsic motivation
4	displacement	9	subjective
5	sobering	10	economic stimulus

Discussion point

Ask students to look at the picture on page 87. Ask them what they can see (a person running through a fountain). Brainstorm any adjectives they would use to talk about the picture and write them on the board (e.g., *refreshing, fun, wet, exhilarating*). Now ask them to look at the unit heading. How do they think this word is connected with the picture? (Water flows, and the man is running through water.) Ask students what else can flow apart from water (e.g., information, ideas, air). Do they think it is a positive or negative word? (It is positive. It relates to smooth movement or progress.)

Now ask students to discuss the questions with a partner. Circulate and note any interesting comments. Invite students to share their ideas with the class.

EXTENSION ACTIVITY

Write the following questions on the board:

1 How much water do you drink each day?

2 How often do you have a shower?

3 How often do you have a bath?

4 How often do you use a washing machine?

Ask students to note down their answers to these questions. Then put them in small groups to compare their answers. They should then answer the following questions: Who uses the most water? Who uses the least water? How can we reduce the amount of water we use every day?

Vocabulary preview

Ask students to read the sentences carefully before they attempt to fill in the gaps. Explain that they will encounter this vocabulary in the listening text that follows this section. They can refer to their dictionaries to help them if necessary. Students can then compare their answers with a partner before feeding back to the class.

EXTENSION ACTIVITY

To further expand their vocabulary relating to water, write the following lists on the board:

1 a reservoir, a well, a strait, a dam

2 a river, a stream, a creek, a bog

3 to sip, to splash, to spray, to sprinkle

4 a mouth, a bed, a bank, a reef

Ask them to work with a partner and identify which word is different in each list, and why. Check answers as a class:

1 *a strait*: a natural passage of water connecting two seas/lakes; the other words relate to manmade control of water

2 *a bog*: wet, muddy ground; the other words relate to moving water

3 *to sip*: to drink fluid in small amounts; the other words relate to deliberately moving water

4 *a reef*: a ridge of rock, coral, or sand just below the surface of the sea; the other words relate to rivers rather than the sea

Now ask students to check the differences in meaning between the three remaining words in each list. They can use a dictionary to help them. Check answers with the whole class.

LISTENING 1 Not worth a dam

Before you listen

Write the word *dam* on the board. Ask students to define it (if they did the *Extension activity* in the *Vocabulary preview* section, they should know this). If they need help, explain that it is a man-made barrier constructed across a waterway to control the flow or raise the level of water. Ask students why a dam might be constructed. Write their ideas on the board.

1 Ask students to discuss the words and phrases with a partner, then share their ideas with the class. Add any new ideas relating to why dams are built to the board, e.g., *dams create reservoirs which allow us to have water available in the right places, dams can provide water for growing crops (irrigation) and for farm animals, they can also be used to generate*

hydroelectric power (a form of renewable energy), and they can help to prevent flooding. Check students understand that the other phrases relate to the potential negative impact of dams.

2 Now ask students to complete the text. They can then check their answers in pairs before feeding back to the class.

ANSWERS

1 irrigation
2 hydroelectric power
3 renewable energy
4 significant controversy
5 environmental costs
6 river ecosystems

Listening

Ask students to look at the *Academic keywords* box. Check that they understand the meanings and that they can pronounce the words correctly. Then ask them to read the questions. Play the audio so they can answer them. You may need to play the audio at the end twice to give students time to note how she finishes her talk. Check answers with the whole class.

AUDIO SCRIPT 2.17

Representative: Good afternoon, members of the committee. Thank you for giving me the opportunity to come and speak to you, as I know you are all very busy. As a representative of the local environmental association, I am here to ask you to reconsider the proposed new dam project. We believe that our government does not have the money to spend on the initial investment.

We also have objections to the dam for the following reasons: Firstly, we believe that the dam will be a disaster for many villages that are alongside the banks of the river where the dam will be built. Secondly, we believe that the dam represents a threat to local wildlife, especially aquatic wildlife. Thirdly, we consider that water would be better stored underground. And finally, we believe that there are better ways to generate energy than building this construction which will ruin our beautiful landscape.

I would like to say a few words about each of these reasons if the committee will permit me. First of all, about the cost of building this dam. We've all heard the argument that it will be a big economic stimulus so it's worth the cost. However, here's the key question: where is the money going to come from? We've been hearing from the government for some time now that there isn't enough money to finance new projects, and that times are tough. So why are we even contemplating a project with an initial investment of more than 40 million dollars? Will this mean our taxes will go up? A hydroelectric dam like the one being suggested is a massive project, and our government just can't afford it. Next, we've been told that local people will benefit from this project—the dam will bring more money and jobs to the area, and so on. But let's look at the other side for a moment. There are many examples of large dam projects displacing local people, sometimes thousands of local people, from their homes. The plans for this dam are no different. The reservoir created by the dam will flood areas up-river, areas with people living, farming, and working in them. This will displace these residents, causing unemployment and economic hardship. The World Commission on Dams, a World Bank-sponsored initiative, estimates that 40 to 80 million people have been displaced by dams. We believe that this dam will continue that trend. Clearly, local people will suffer more than they benefit from this project.

Now, I'm sure you've all heard the claims that the dam will be constructed on environmentally friendly principles, so that the impact on the environment will be minimal. Well, that depends on how you define *minimal*. The statistics are sobering. Sixty per cent of the length of the world's large river systems is affected by dams. Dams are a major reason for the loss of freshwater fish. Around a third of freshwater fish species are classified as extinct, endangered, or vulnerable. Also, when the river floods its banks, this can result in the loss of wildlife that previously inhabited that land. It is worth mentioning that a significant portion of this wildlife is not displaced (as is the case with human beings), but actually killed. I don't know about you, but I wouldn't call that a *minimal* impact. Another argument in favor of dams is that they are an efficient way to store water. However, we would argue that underground water-storage is a superior alternative, as storing water above ground risks contamination, evaporation, damage to ecosystems, and flooding. For instance, according to the International Rivers Association, around 7% of the total amount of fresh water consumed by all human activities is lost from reservoirs due to evaporation.

These are compelling reasons not to build the dam for water storage purposes. As for a source of electricity, we have all seen the predictions made in terms of hydroelectricity from this dam. It's true that it will generate a huge amount of power. Nonetheless, we would like to point out that wind and solar energy are two other options which would have much less effect on the local population, economy, and wildlife, and therefore should be considered.

I realize that my time may be up, and that the committee needs to hear from other people about the situation as well. I am prepared to present plenty more data, and full and complete documentation from independent sources that supports everything I have told you here today. I urge you to reconsider this project for the good of our people, for the good of our community, and for the good of our land. Thank you for your attention.

ANSWERS

1 She is speaking to committee members.
2 She is asking participants to reconsider a dam project.
3 She gives four reasons: building costs; displacement of the local population; environmental damage; and ineffective water storage.
4 (I urge you to reconsider this project for the good of our people, for the good of our community, and for the good of our land.) Thank you for your attention.

Critical thinking skill

Exam tip

This task is similar to the IELTS part 4 listening paper where students hear a monologue on a topic. The question type is also similar to an IELTS question where students are given a list of options and have to choose which ones are mentioned. If you have students preparing for IELTS, explain that it's important that they read the question carefully to identify exactly what they are listening for. They also need to make sure they input the right number of options; writing more or fewer options would result in the student losing marks.

Ask students to read the information in the *Identifying counter-arguments* box and check that they understand it. Remind them that whenever they formulate an argument in their academic work, they should anticipate potential counter-arguments and try to disprove them. This will show they have considered the topic from all angles before reaching their conclusion.

1 Ask students to read the seven arguments. Play the audio again so that they can check the arguments they hear. Check answers with the whole class.

ANSWERS

Sentences 1, 3, 4, 5, and 7 should be checked.

2 Ask students to match the arguments, then check answers with the whole class.

ANSWERS

a 5　b 1　c 3　d 7　e 4

3 Have students work in pairs to discuss the speaker's counter-arguments. You may need to play the audio again if students are struggling to recall what was said. Check answers with the whole class.

POSSIBLE ANSWERS

1 The speaker says that the costs are unaffordable. Government financial resources are stretched, and there would be a risk of increased taxation to generate the funds needed for the project.
2 The speaker gives statistics to support her argument. She says that 60% of river systems are affected by dams, and that many species are threatened as a result.
3 The speaker states that water storage in dams is inefficient, since a portion of it evaporates. Underground water storage is a better alternative.

Developing critical thinking

Ask students to discuss the questions in groups. Circulate and monitor, noting any interesting comments. Invite students to share their ideas with the class as a follow-up.

LISTENING 2 The concept of flow

Before you listen

Discuss these questions as a class. Write students' ideas on the board.

Listening

Ask students to look at the *Academic keywords* box. Check that they understand the words and can pronounce them correctly. Then ask students to look at the diagram. Play the audio so that students can answer the questions. Check answers with the whole class.

AUDIO SCRIPT 2.18

Professor: Good afternoon, everyone, Welcome to the first lecture of our new module called Positive Psychology, which as you know is one of the newest branches to emerge in our field. While many other branches tend to focus on dysfunction and abnormal behavior, positive psychology is centered on how to help people become happier.

I would like to begin by asking you a question: What makes a happy life?

I'd like you to think about how you would answer this question. When you have an answer, I'd like you to tell the person sitting next to you.

Now I'm going to give you one possible answer. *A happy life is one that is characterized by complete absorption in what one does.* How does this compare with what you and your partner said?

This answer comes from the work of Mihaly Csikszentmihalyi and the theory of flow. Csikszentmihalyi is a psychologist who has spent most of his professional life on the study of what makes people happy and how we can attain happiness. His interest in this began when he met people who had lived through traumatic wartime experiences, but who had survived and seemed happy, whereas other survivors of war could not seem to get over their negative experiences. He wondered what could explain this difference. Csikszentmihalyi put forward the theory that happiness is not caused by external events, but is more a result of our perception of them. As such, we have to seek happiness in order to find it. However, this does not mean that we should relentlessly pursue pleasure! Csikszentmihalyi came to the conclusion that our happiest moments are those when we are in a state of flow.

The theory of flow can be summarized as a state of mind or a state of experience that we feel when we are totally involved in what we are doing. The inspiration to begin researching this theory was provided by Csikszentmihalyi's interest in art. He noticed the way in which artists worked in the studio. They completely lost track of time, they didn't notice they were hungry—although they were tired, and they worked for days without stopping. Anyone I have spoken to who has experienced this state of concentration has found it difficult to explain. The best metaphor I have heard is that it's like being in a river and the flow of the water carries you away.

Let's consider how one can enter such a state.

Csikszentmihalyi published *Flow: The Psychology of Optimal Experience* in 1990, and in it he identified six factors that accompany a state of flow:

First, there is intense and focused concentration on the action you are performing—there is a high amount of intrinsic motivation here. It must be an activity that you really want to do.

Secondly, your actions and awareness merge—that means your concentration is so strong that you are only aware of what you are doing and nothing else. Consequently, and this is the third factor, you lose reflective self-consciousness—meaning that you do not think of yourself at all, only the action.

The fourth factor is that you have a sense of control over the activity—you are very aware that your actions are playing a vital part in its execution.

The fifth factor is that your subjective experience of time is altered—that means you have no sense of time whatsoever. Finally, your experience of the activity is intrinsically rewarding—what you are doing gives you great pleasure. Remember that *intrinsic* means an action is satisfying in itself and not affected by any external factor. These aspects may appear individually when you are involved in an activity, but ONLY when there is a combination of ALL six can you enter into a state of flow. When one is in flow, one works at one's full capacity.

One thing worth noting here is that you cannot force yourself to enter a state of flow. It simply happens when the conditions are right. It is likely to occur when you are actively involved in an action for intrinsic reasons. Note that passive actions, such as watching TV, cannot produce a state of flow, as you have to be actively involved.

Flow: The Psychology of Optimal Experience also stipulates three conditions that have to be met in order to allow you to enter a state of flow:

Number one is that you have to be focused on an activity with clear goals ... very clear objectives. For example, in gymnastics you not only have to vault the apparatus, but also land with your feet perfectly positioned inside the lines on the floor.

The second is that you need to have immediate feedback on the action in case there are any changes to the conditions; this allows the person to adjust their performance to maintain the flow state. If we take the high jump as another sports example, the competitor must know that they have two attempts at one particular height—if the first attempt fails, they have to raise their performance on the final jump or be eliminated.

Finally, there has to be a balance of challenge and skills. If the task were too difficult, it would cause you to feel anxious and block the state of flow. However, the same would happen if the task were too easy—flow could not occur due to the fact that you would consider it boring.

POSSIBLE ANSWERS

1 intense and focused concentration
2 actions and awareness merge
3 lose reflective self-consciousness
4 sense of control over the activity
5 subjective experience of time is altered

---

6 experience of the activity is intrinsically rewarding
According to the speaker, flow theory is about a set of conditions for becoming completely involved in an experience.

Critical thinking skill

Ask students to read the information in the *Visual aids and diagrams* box. They may be aware that use of visuals in lectures helps to keep the attention of the audience. They should bear this in mind when writing their own presentations.

1 Ask students to look at the visual aids and decide what each conveys. Brainstorm their ideas with the whole class. Then play the audio and ask them to make notes.

POSSIBLE ANSWERS

1 Positive psychology is centered on people becoming happier (instead of dysfunction and abnormal behavior).
2 A happy life is one that is characterized by complete absorption in what one does.
3 Passive actions, such as watching TV, cannot produce a state of flow—you have to be actively involved.
4 The three conditions to achieve flow

---

2 Play the last part of the lecture, then brainstorm suggestions for visual aids with the class. You could also ask individual students to draw their suggested visual aid on the board.

AUDIO SCRIPT 2.19

Professor: *Flow: The Psychology of Optimal Experience* also stipulates three conditions that have to be met in order to allow you to enter a state of flow:

Number one is that you have to be focused on an activity with clear goals ... very clear objectives. For example, in gymnastics you not only have to vault the apparatus, but also land with your feet perfectly positioned inside the lines on the floor.

The second is that you need to have immediate feedback on the action in case there are any changes to the conditions; this allows the person to adjust their performance to maintain the flow state. If we take the high jump as another sports example, the competitor must know that they have two attempts at one particular height—if the first attempt fails, they have to raise their performance on the final jump or be eliminated.

Finally, there has to be a balance of challenge and skills. If the task were too difficult, it would cause you to feel anxious and block the state of flow. However, the same would happen if the task were too easy—flow could not occur due to the fact that you would consider it boring. Now, let's consider this example.

Flow

POSSIBLE ANSWER

Other visual aids to support the last part of the lecture could include featuring images associated with the concepts of goals, feedback, and balance.

Developing critical thinking

1 Ask students to discuss the questions in a group. Then have them share their ideas with the class.

2 Students discuss the questions in groups. Remind them to think about both listening texts. When discussing information flow, ask them to think about the role of the Internet. Circulate and note any interesting comments. Invite students to share their ideas with the class as a follow-up.

Language development: Irregular plurals

Ask students to read the information in the *Irregular plurals* box. Remind them that in some cases they will need to learn the plural forms by checking the word in a dictionary, as they are not simply created with the addition of an -*s*.

1 Ask students to form the plurals of the words. Encourage them to use their dictionaries. They can then check their answers with a partner before feeding back to the class.

ANSWERS

1 hypotheses	10 metamorphoses
2 series	11 stimuli
3 species	12 conundrums
4 halves	13 aircraft
5 bases	14 bogs
6 kilos	15 youths
7 heroes	16 reservoirs
8 audiences	17 statistics
9 proximities	18 knowledge

2 Ask students to form the singular of the words. Check the answers with the class.

ANSWERS

1 no singular form	5 no singular form
2 criterion	6 no singular form
3 no singular form	7 phenomenon
4 knife	8 no singular form

3 Ask students to read the sentences and circle the correct words. If they need to, they can refer to their dictionaries for help. They can then check their answers in pairs before feeding back to the class. For the answer to question 1, point out that the word *data* is plural, but most native English speakers will actually use this word in structures that imply it is a singular noun. Academics usually

use the word in the plural form as it is part of their everyday working lives. *Datum* is the singular form of *data*.

ANSWERS

1 suggest	6 produces
2 have closed	7 it
3 both are possible	8 both are possible
4 are	9 are
5 are	10 both are possible

Language development: Words in context—working with concordance data

Ask students to read the information in the *Words in context—working with concordance data* box. Highlight the fact that concordances can really help to show common collocations and uses of words. This is useful to language learners as it can help them understand how they can use the word effectively in their own speech or writing.

Students should answer the questions about the word *flow*. Check answers with the whole class.

ANSWERS

1 verb or noun
2 *continuous, free*
3 *correspondence, noise, information, funds, fuel, tunes, air, blood, cash, commerce*
4 *the/a + flow + of + noun*
5 *a flow of cash* and *the flow of commerce*

This is a good place to use the video resource *Volcanic flow*. It is located in the Video resources section of the digital component. Alternatively, remind students about the video so they can do this at home.

Extension activity

Ask students to work in pairs and choose three of the expressions listed with the word *flow* from the concordance data. Ask them to write sentences using these expressions. Monitor and help as necessary. Once students have finished, elicit one for each collocation from the table, if possible.

SPEAKING Making an advertisement supported by visuals

Pronunciation skill

Ask students to read the information in the *Intonation to express hesitation and doubt* box. Remind them that they cannot only rely on the words used to decipher the speaker's feelings on a topic as intonation can also provide a lot of information.

1 Write two headings on the board: *agree* and *disagree*. As a class, divide the words in the box into the two groups and write them on the board.

ANSWERS
agree: yes; I guess so; well, OK
disagree: no; I don't think so; I'm not sure

2 Play the audio so that students can hear the different kinds of intonation. They should note down which examples use stronger agreement or disagreement. Check answers with the class, then play the audio again, pausing after each phrase, and drilling the pronunciation with the class and then with individual students.

AUDIO SCRIPT 2.20

1	4
Yes.	Well, OK.
Yes.	Well, OK.
2	5
No.	I don't think so.
No.	I don't think so.
3	6
I guess so.	I'm not sure.
I guess so.	I'm not sure.

ANSWERS
1 a   2 b   3 b   4 a   5 a   6 a

Speaking skill

Ask students to read the information in the *Softening criticism* box and check that they understand it.

Cultural awareness

In American and British culture, it is important to be polite when you are criticizing others. However, in other cultures, people are free to be more direct and can openly criticize generally without fear of offending others.

In some cultures, people tend to avoid criticism in order not to offend others. Remind students that even if their culture avoids criticism of others, when studying in an international academic context, they will need to be able to criticize other peoples' opinions, but that doing this politely and tactfully may help them to do this more readily.

1 Students should soften the criticisms individually. Refer them back to the box to help them.

POSSIBLE ANSWERS
1 You may have done the wrong exercise.
2 It seems to me that your conclusion is confusing.
3 I find it difficult to understand your accent.
4 It seems we aren't communicating well.
5 I wonder if it might be better for you to do it again.
6 You might not have quoted the source correctly.

2 Ask students to share their answers with a partner and practice saying them aloud.

3 Ask students to work with a partner to prepare the phrases. Circulate and monitor. Invite students to write their suggested phrases on the board. Correct where necessary and drill the phrases with the students.

SPEAKING TASK

Brainstorm and plan

Put students into pairs. Ask them to read the situation. They should then answer the questions. If your students did the first *Extension activity* on page 74, they will have already started to think about issues related to water shortage. Encourage them to build on those ideas.

Invite pairs to share their ideas with the class and write the suggestions for saving water on the board.

Ask students to work individually to decide which strategies they will mention in their advertisement and how they will present the information, both visually and with words.

Speak and share

Put students into small groups so that they can share their ideas. Refer them back to the language on page 94 to help them soften any criticisms they may have. Students should then agree on a final advertisement, and work together to prepare a storyboard and a script. If you like, you could assign this as homework, and they can use PowerPoint to create slides showing their storyboard and one member of the group can read the voiceover script aloud.

Ask groups to present their advertisements. While they present, make a note of any language errors or pronunciation issues, especially intonation, for feedback. Students should then vote on the best advertisement. Use the photocopiable *Unit assignment checklist* on page 96 to assess the students' speaking.

Extra research task

Write the following statement on the board: *Water shortage is a complex and expensive problem to solve.*

Ask students to conduct online research to find concrete material that supports this argument. They should find two or three sources. Ask them to find out which countries have water shortage problems, how they try to solve these problems, and the complexities of the techniques and possible solutions. In the next class, students can share their findings and discuss their opinions on the statement.

STUDY SKILLS Exam techniques

Background information

Many of your students will face exams at some point during their academic career, especially those studying science subjects. These can be particularly nerve-wracking for non-native speakers, as they will not have the time or opportunity to look up any words they do not understand, and may not have time to proofread their work thoroughly before the end of the exam.

Getting started

Ask students to work with a partner to discuss the questions. Invite students to share their ideas with the class.

Scenario

Have students read about Tania and decide which techniques are beneficial. Invite students to share their thoughts with the class.

POSSIBLE ANSWER

I think avoiding other students who make you feel nervous and anxious about exams is beneficial.

Cultural awareness

Attitudes towards cheating vary across cultures, but in English-speaking countries cheating during examinations is not tolerated, so students need to be made aware of this. This means that they will not be allowed to talk during the exams, nor will they be allowed to take notes in or use the Internet. Doing any of these things could result in them receiving 0% for the exam, or in more serious cases they could even be asked to leave the university entirely.

Consider it

Ask students to read the tips about what to do during an exam (not before it). They should check the tips that they use. Don't discuss their ideas at this point as they will have a chance to do this in the following section.

Over to you

Ask students to discuss their ideas with a partner. Ask them to note down additional tips and what they might avoid doing. Circulate and note any interesting ideas. Invite students to share their ideas with the class and write any useful tips on the board.

Exam tip

If you have a group of students who are preparing for a specific exam such as IELTS, you could ask them to look at the *Consider it* tips and ask which of these they think are particularly relevant to that exam. Then ask students to share any additional tips or knowledge they have about the exam in groups. Students should then try to write three or four exam-specific tips. Elicit and share these with the group.

Critical thinking	Identifying strengths in theories and arguments Consistency
Language development	Hedging and boosting Using the correct linker
Pronunciation	Linking and catenation
Speaking	Managing conflict—reformulating and monitoring

Discussion point

Direct students' attention to the picture on page 97. Ask them what they can see (male penguins using mating calls to attract females). Ask them how this image is connected to the unit title, *Conflict* (it shows an example of conflict being played out in the animal world).

Ask students to discuss the questions with a partner. They may find it difficult to think of examples for question 1, so you might need to prompt them with some examples to start them off (e.g., human vs. human = wars, marital breakdown, boxing match, etc.; nature vs. nature = predators catching their prey, weeds destroying a garden, etc.; machine vs. machine = radio signals interfering with electrical equipment, an airplane autopilot overriding manual controls, etc.).

Vocabulary preview

1   Ask students to complete the sentences with the words in the box. They should try to complete the exercise without using their dictionaries so that they can practice using context to decipher meaning. Students can then check their answers in pairs before feeding back to the class.

ANSWERS
1 alluding to; criticize   5 loyalty
2 aftermath   6 struggle
3 rivalry; animosity   7 accusation
4 violent

2   Discuss these questions with the whole class.

ANSWERS
Negative: criticize, aftermath, animosity, violent, struggle, accusation
Positive or neutral: alluding to, rivalry, loyalty

This is a good place to use the video resource *The warrior gene*. It is located in the Video resources section of the digital component. Alternatively, remind students about the video so they can do this at home.

Write the following positive words connected with conflict on the board: *negotiation, reconciliation, compromise, alleviate, arbitrate, resolution, ceasefire, consultation*.

Ask students to work in pairs and use a dictionary to help them do the following:

1 Find out what kind of word each one is (verb, noun, etc.).

2 Can they build on each to create a word family? (e.g., *negotiation* = noun, *negotiate* = verb)

3 What is the exact definition for each word?

4 Can they write an example sentence for each?

Ask students to share their findings with the class during feedback.

LISTENING 1 Conflict of interest

Before you listen

1   Ask students to read the abstract carefully and decide on the best title. Discuss students' ideas with the whole class.

ANSWER   I think (a)
b (Although a covers part of the topic, b is the more comprehensive summary.)

2   Brainstorm examples on the board with the whole class. If students struggle to think of anything, you could suggest the following examples: supports the statement = when several athletes in a race take performance enhancing drugs, meaning the drug-free athletes come last; disproves the statement = when; someone finds some money on the street and hands it into the police, and they later receive a substantial reward.

Refer students to the *Academic keywords* box. Check that they understand the words and can pronounce them correctly.

Listening

Ask students to read the headings in the notes. You may need to check their understanding of *consequential* (following as a result or effect) and *scholarship* (a payment made to support a student's education awarded due to achievement). Then play the audio while students make a note of why the words and phrases were written down. Check answers with the class, then put students into pairs so that they can practice summarizing the sections. Circulate and monitor while they do so, noting any good examples. Invite individual students to share their summaries with the class.

AUDIO SCRIPT 2.21

Presenter: Hi, everybody. Thanks for coming. Thanks for being here. Wow. This conference, it's great, isn't it? I've been having a great time so far. How about you?

I'd like to start my talk with a little test for you. I want you to imagine that a good friend of yours has just had a baby. Unfortunately, the baby is rather unattractive. Very unattractive, in fact. Your friend asks you, "Isn't she the most gorgeous baby you have ever seen?"

What do you say? Honesty, that's important for you. On the other hand, you don't want to hurt your friend's feelings. You've got a dilemma here.

Now, this is a rather small dilemma, and it's probably easy for most people to solve it. But what about situations like the following? Imagine you are responsible for selecting a winner of a scholarship. A good friend of yours applies for the job. Your friend is qualified, but then another applicant who is even more qualified applies for the same scholarship. The second applicant probably needs the scholarship even more than your friend. It is your decision alone. Who do you give the scholarship to?

These are all examples of moral or ethical dilemmas. There are different ways that we can address them. For the rest of my presentation, I'd like to offer you frameworks and theories on just how we can deal with a moral dilemma or conflict. Thinking through these theories can help us, I believe, make the best choices when we have these kinds of difficult situations. Now, don't be intimidated by the big words I'm going to use—each one of these theories I'll explain as clearly as possible.

For example, you can look at resolving ethical conflicts using a consequential theory or non-consequential theory. As the words indicate, these all have to do with the consequences of our actions. Let's begin firstly with consequential theories. A consequential theory states that your actions are judged by the results. An action that produces a good result must be morally right. If the action doesn't produce a good result, then it must be wrong.

So, for example, imagine a factory that is polluting the environment. If we close the factory, then we will have cleaner air and water. So closing the factory is the correct thing to do as it produces a good result.

Pause there for a second. What is a good result? Is a good result something that merely is good for you and your own interests? Or is it good if it produces the greatest ratio of good for the most people? If it's only good for you, then this is an egotistical consequential view. If it produces good for the most people, it's a utilitarian consequential view.

Compare these questions to those posed by a non-consequential theory. Non-consequential theories state that other factors than the outcome, other factors than the consequence, must be taken into account when faced with an ethical dilemma.

Going back to our factory example. If closing the factory means that lots of people will lose their jobs, and that a whole community might suffer economically, then this must be considered and weighed against the outcome of cleaner air and water.

There are different kinds of non-consequential theory. One is the Golden Rule. This states that you should treat others as you would wish to be treated, regardless of the outcome. Remember that scholarship we talked about earlier? How would you feel if you lost it because the committee president gave it to his best friend? Bad? Then don't let it happen if you're on a committee deciding scholarships.

Another non-consequential theory states that a decision is good as long as you respect and follow certain duties, called the *prima facie* duties. These could include justice, generosity, or loyalty.

Faced with difficult choices and internal conflict, these theories, these frameworks, I believe, clearly help us. This is the first step to long-term success. Now, let me go more into depth on …

POSSIBLE ANSWERS

ugly baby—This is an example of a situation in which it is difficult to tell a friend that they have an ugly baby because you wouldn't want to hurt his/her feelings.

applicant scholarship—This is mentioned in relation to another ethical dilemma. If you had to present a scholarship to one of two people, and one of those people is a good friend of yours, then it becomes more difficult to decide who to award it to.

consequential and non-consequential—Ethical dilemmas can be resolved by following the consequential or non-consequential theory. This means that a consequential theory assumes you will be judged by the results of your decision. Non-consequential theory involves decisions in which factors other than the outcome become important.

closing the factory—In any decision-making, there should be an assessment of priorities, as given through the example of closing a factory. In that case, the decision should either be in favor of improving the environment, or preserving the jobs of a group of people.

justice, generosity, loyalty—These are examples of when a decision taken is acceptable, as long as the principles of justice, generosity, or loyalty are kept in mind.

Critical thinking skill

Ask students to read the information in the *Identifying strengths in theories and arguments* box. Remind them that when presenting arguments in their own essays and presentations, they need to use sound research to back up their ideas, and this means they need to find information or sources that involve strong arguments.

The questions in the table will help students to judge whether the information they have found involves strong arguments.

Encourage students to make a note of the three nouns at the bottom of the box. These are useful words when students need to criticize weak arguments.

1 Ask students to read the sentences. Then play the audio again so that they can fill in the gaps. Students can check their answers in pairs before feeding back to the class.

> **ANSWERS**
> 1 utilitarian 3 egotistical
> 2 golden rule 4 *prima facie*

2 Have students match the criticisms to the theories. Again, they should check their answers in pairs before feeding back to the class.

> **ANSWERS**
> a 2 b 3 c 4 d 1

Developing critical thinking

Ask students to discuss the questions in groups. Circulate and monitor, noting any interesting points that students can share with the class as a follow-up.

LISTENING 2 "The Sporting Spirit"

Before you listen

1 Ask students to discuss the questions with a partner. During feedback, write down any famous rivalries on the board. Ask students which person or team they support in each example, and why.

2 Ask students to read the information in the box, which provides background on an essay written by George Orwell. Then have them answer the questions.

> **Background information**
> George Orwell was the pen name of Eric Arthur Blair, born in India in 1903, but raised in Britain. Orwell became a famous writer, focusing on topics of social injustice and totalitarianism. Some of his books include *Down and Out in Paris and London*, which looked at the lives of poorer people living in those cities, and *1984*, a novel based on a totalitarian state where Big Brother is always watching everyone.

> **ANSWERS**
> 1 negative
> 2 attack: lash out at
> criticize: lambast
> 3 It sounds as though it will give a one-sided view.

Listening

Highlight the fact that students are about to listen to a seminar debate, so there will be several voices to tune in to in the listening text. Draw their attention to the *Academic keywords* box. Check that they understand them and can pronounce them correctly. Encourage them to use their dictionaries if they are struggling. Then ask students to read the list of events carefully. Play the audio so that they can order them. Students can then check their answers in pairs before feeding back to the class.

> **AUDIO SCRIPT 2.22**
>
> **Professor:** OK, guys. Let's get started, shall we? I asked you to prepare arguments for or against the statement: *Sport is an unfailing cause of ill will.*
>
> **Class:** Yes./OK./Yes.
>
> **Professor:** I also gave you an article called "The Sporting Spirit" written by the British author George Orwell as background reading and asked you to find more sources to use as support for your reasons. Who would like to start?
>
> **Student 1:** Well, I'm going to give a summary of Orwell's stance, but first …
>
> **Student 2:** Yes, first we thought we needed to clarify the context of the article. It was written in 1945 in response to a soccer tour of Great Britain by the Soviet Union side Dynamo Moscow. This was the aftermath of the Second World War when there was a growing mutual mistrust between the two countries. Um … we researched newspaper articles from around the time preceding the tour. And … according to one newspaper the event was inappropriate, as it was right after World War II. Another paper reported that using sports as a tool of international relations was dangerous. So, we can see that there was quite a lot of negativity before the tour took place and that many people didn't think it was a good idea for the two countries to compete against each other in a sporting event.
>
> **Professor:** Go on.
>
> **Student 1:** Right. So, Orwell wrote the essay after the tour, and he said that it created animosity on both sides—by this he means mutual bad feeling. He said that soccer was a source of passion, but it could be negative passion. To support this, he mentions negative incidents produced in two of the matches: violent conduct from players on both sides, the crowd booing the referee and the players, and there were also accusations of cheating from both the British and the Russians. He doesn't say anything positive about the tour … I mean … the Russians even went home early before they played their final match. They walked out, in a way.
>
> **Professor:** OK, so we have an international soccer event that seems to have caused bad feelings on both sides. What evidence have you found to support or go against the statement that the sport was the cause of the ill will or bad feeling as you say?

Student 3: You know, I think I can see two different points there. I feel Orwell's getting at what competitive soccer does to the players and how it influences the spectators. In a negative sense, I mean. It was something he said later in the article. Where is it? Ah, here it is … he talks about crowds having to be controlled by the police, and incidents of spectators running onto the field and harming the players. I see his point about soccer "provoking vicious passions in the general public."

Student 2: He also alludes to a lack of sporting spirit between the players by saying that "Serious sport has nothing to do with fair play" and that sport being competitive, "You play to win" and the game "has little meaning unless you do your utmost to win." He seems to be saying that it's all about winning and nothing else. Could that have been the cause of the bad feeling during the soccer tour?

Student 1: I think both of you make good points there. If we think about soccer in general all over the world, it does tend to give us lots of incidents of both player violence and crowd violence, which you don't find in other sports quite as much. And, I can also say that I agree with the point that he makes about being disgraced if you lose, causing bad feeling—I mean—in soccer whether it's the UEFA Champions League® or the FIFA World Cup™—everyone plays to win, and it's a disaster when your team's eliminated.

Student 2: Yeah, it's like we want it all or nothing at all. We have to win—we can't accept that playing well is enough.

Student 3: I did consider that, so what I did was look for something that would suggest otherwise. In my research, I came across Pierre de Coubertain's speech from 1892. This speech was made in support of the revival of the ancient Greek Olympics. He states that "The important thing in life is not the triumph but the struggle, the essential thing is not to have conquered but to have fought well." He saw the revival of the Olympic Games as important in supporting his philosophical ideal for athletic competition, which was that the competition itself, the struggle to overcome your opponent, was more important than winning. You see, here we have what sports should be ideally.

Student 2: Exactly! That is what it should be, but why isn't it like that in practice? Is it just human nature?

Student 1: Listen, guys. I'm beginning to think that maybe it isn't sports that causes these rivalries. I was just thinking that … that sports give us the chance to express our rivalries—you know the conflicts that are already there. The sporting event just brings it out in the open.

Student 2: Ah, OK then. Do you think that he really wanted to criticize patriotism—not sports? He stated that the rise of serious sports was bound to the rise of nationalism. His own words are, "If you wanted to add to the vast fund of ill will existing in the world at this moment, you could hardly do it better than by a series of football matches." The examples he uses are matches between Russians and Poles, Germans and Czechs, and Britain and India, who were obviously bitter rivals at the time.

Student 3: OK, so you're saying that this nationalism is already there and comes out during sporting events. I mean, Orwell admits that sports aren't essentially nationalistic. He also declares that sports are not the cause of international rivalry, but it's rather *an effect* of the real causes that produce nationalism. This would back up what you've just said.

Student 2: So, by joining the two together in this article, could he be confusing what sports can be and the real essence of sports?

Professor: Can you reach a conclusion as to what the essence of sports is? Try by defining the word *sportsmanship*.

Student 3: We believe that sportsmanship describes taking part in competition for enjoyment only. It involves a sense of fairness and respect for our opponents. This is certainly what sports should be.

Professor: So, is sport the unfailing cause of ill will?

Student 1: Well, it's really Orwell's article that helps us come to our conclusion. He begins by stating that "sport is an unfailing cause of ill will." Yet, we feel that he contradicts himself in the closing part when he writes, "I do not, of course, suggest that sport is one of the main causes of international rivalry." He starts by saying it's an unfailing cause and concludes by stating that it's not one of the main causes. We feel that nationalism and tribalism can come out during sports events. But, the cause isn't the sport itself—the rivalries are already there.

Students 2 and 3: Agreed.

Professor: Well, thank you to all of you for putting your reasoned arguments forward in today's session. Now, we can go on to deal with …

Critical thinking skill

Ask students to read the information in the *Consistency* box. Check that they understand the importance of consistency in essays or presentations. Alert them to the fact that acknowledging opposing points of view is also fine in a consistent argument, as long as counter-arguments to this opposing view are also presented.

1 Ask students to listen to the audio again, read the sentences, and decide if they are consistent with Orwell's conclusion, contradict the conclusion, or are incidental.

2 Ask students to identify the example of inconsistency in Orwell's argument that the students give.

Exact wording of answer may vary. The answer comes from this section of the audio script: … Yet, we feel that he contradicts himself in the closing part when he writes "I do not, of course, suggest that sport is one of the main causes of international rivalry." He starts by saying it's an unfailing cause and concludes by stating that it's not one of the main causes. We feel that nationalism and tribalism can come out during sports events. But, the cause isn't the sport itself—the rivalries are already there.

Developing critical thinking

1 Ask students to work in groups to discuss the questions. Other international events that they may mention could include music festivals or competitions (e.g., The Eurovision Song Contest), religious festivals, or pilgrimages (e.g.,The Hajj).

2 Remind students to think back to *Listening 1* as well as *Listening 2*. They should then discuss the questions in their groups. Circulate and monitor, noting any interesting comments. Invite students to share their ideas with the class.

EXTENSION ACTIVITY

Write the question, *Is nationalism good or bad?* on the board. Then write two columns with the headings *good* and *bad*. Brainstorm ideas and evidence that support both sides of the argument (e.g., bad—*it can lead to an increase in racism that can result in conflict*; good—*it creates a sense of togetherness and helps form a cultural identity*). Then ask students what their opinions are and why. You could ask them to conduct more research for homework to discuss in the following lesson.

Language development: Hedging and boosting

Ask students to read the information in the *Hedging and boosting* box carefully.

Background information

Hedging has become an important part of academic writing style. It does not show weakness in a student's argument, but rather performs one or more of the following functions:

1 Makes a statement less strong to help avoid any immediate opposition or counter-arguments.

2 Helps the students to show lack of clarity, perhaps because the research they are quoting is not 100% reliable in their opinion.

3 Allows the student to appear more humble and less arrogant, meaning that the reader or the audience will be more open to what they have to say.

In contrast, boosting can be used when a student is really sure about an argument or idea and is passionate about it.

1 Ask students to work individually to categorize the expressions. Check answers with the whole class.

ANSWERS

More assertive: certainly, without a doubt, for certain, inevitably, categorically, unquestionably
Less assertive: apparently, in some respects, partially, as a general rule, seemingly, in a sense, likely

2 Allow time for students to alter the sentences. Refer them back to the language in the *Hedging and boosting* box to help them. They can then check their answers in pairs before feeding back to the class.

ANSWERS

1 Now, this is a small dilemma, and it's **unquestionably** easy for most people to solve it.
2 An action that produces a good result **may** be morally right.
3 Faced with difficult choices and internal conflict, these frameworks, I believe, help us **in some respects**.
4 We **should** remind ourselves that without electricity, nothing would work.
5 The threat is out there, and it's **seemingly** real.

3 Students should work individually to rewrite these sentences according to their own views. Invite individual students to write their sentences on the board for analysis.

Language development: Using the correct linker

Ask students to read the information in the *Using the correct linker* box. Highlight the fact that these linkers are easily confused so it's important that they understand the meaning and use of each one. Encourage them to write them down in their vocabulary notebooks, with a definition and example of how they are used.

1 Ask students to underline the correct linkers. They can then check their answers in pairs before feeding back to the class.

ANSWERS

1 Firstly	4 On the contrary
2 at first	5 on the other hand
3 at last	

2 Ask students now to write their own sentences using the linkers. Invite individual students to write their ideas on the board during feedback.

SPEAKING Role-playing mini-conflict situations

Pronunciation skill

Ask students to read the information in the *Linking and catenation* box. Model the two example sentences to show them how meaning can sometimes be confused when catenation is used.

1 Drill the six words in the box as a class, then ask students to work individually to find the pronunciation of the words within the sentences. Check answers with the whole class, asking individual students to read the sentences aloud so you can check their pronunciation.

> **ANSWERS**
> 1 I'd like to offer framework**s and** theories.
> 2 I see your point **ab**out this.
> 3 That exam was awful—if I pas**s it**, I'll be amazed.
> 4 Nothing a**t all**.
> 5 The team walk**ed out** of the stadium.
> 6 I'd like to say tha**t I** agree.

2 Play the audio so that the students can hear the American English speaker. Try to encourage the students to replicate the pronunciation they hear. Play the audio a second time and pause after each sentence so that you can drill the students.

> **AUDIO SCRIPT 2.23**
> 1 I'd like to offer framework<u>s and</u> theories.
> 2 I see your poin<u>t ab</u>out this.
> 3 That exam was awful—if I pas<u>s it</u>, I'll be amazed.
> 4 Nothing a<u>t all</u>.
> 5 The team walk<u>ed out</u> of the stadium.
> 6 I'd like to say tha<u>t I</u> agree.

Speaking skill

Ask students to read the information in the *Managing conflict—reformulating and monitoring* box. Highlight the fact that these expressions are very useful in seminar discussions and they should try to use them where possible.

1 Play the audio so that students can answer the questions. Check their answers with the whole class.

> **AUDIO SCRIPT 2.24**
> A: … so I'm proposing that we use the extra funding towards improving the cafeteria and green spaces on campus. How many people are in favour?
> B: Hold on a moment … so you're saying that none of the money should go towards improving arts facilities?

> A: Well, technically, arts facilities are the responsibility of the individual arts departments, and this funding was intended for making general improvements on campus that will benefit *all* students, not only arts students …
> B: As a matter of fact, my proposal *would* benefit all students. If we use the money to build an arts centre, it could be used for all kinds of activities … for example, social events, meetings of various societies …
> A: In other words, it would have the same function as the Hodgson building, which we already have. I just think we need a better cafeteria more urgently. And the green spaces are in a really bad state …
> B: OK, why don't we have a vote on it?
> A: Sure, that sounds like a good idea. So, all those in favour …

> **POSSIBLE ANSWER**
> The students disagree on how to spend the extra funding money. They agree to have a vote on it.

2 Play the audio again, and encourage students to make a note of how the speakers reformulate and monitor.

> **ANSWERS**
> Some examples of reformulation and monitoring from the discourse:
> So you're saying …
> Well, technically …
> As a matter of fact, …
> In other words, …

3 Ask students to read the first three lines in a conflict about loud music. Refer them back to the language for reformulating and monitoring, then ask them to continue the exchange with a partner. Circulate and monitor, noting any good examples that can be shared with the class during the feedback stage.

SPEAKING TASK

Brainstorm

Ask students to read the four conflict situations, three of which are centered around students. Discuss the questions as a class and find out if your students have any experience of these types of conflict.

Plan

1 Put students into groups of three and ask them to choose a conflict from the *Brainstorm* section.

2 Allow plenty of time for students to prepare for their conflict. Ask them to look back at the

language in the unit, especially expressions for hedging, reformulating, and correcting. Remind the arbitrators that they need to evaluate the strength of both Student A's and Student B's arguments, and they will need to point these out in a polite way during the role play.

Speak and share

Groups now perform their role plays. Circulate and monitor, noting good use of expressions and any particularly good arbitrators. Provide any feedback on language and performance.

Put groups together so they can compare what happened in their conflicts and discuss their resolutions. During this stage, monitor and take language notes. Use the photocopiable *Unit assignment checklist* on page 97 to assess the students' speaking.

Extra research task

Write the following statements on the board: *1 Conflict can bring about positive outcomes. 2 Conflict is destructive.* Put students into pairs. Student A should research the first statement and be prepared to provide evidence and examples to support it. Student B should research the second statement, also preparing evidence and examples to support it. In the next lesson, pairs should present their research to each other and try to persuade each other to agree with them. Remind students to utilize language they have learnt in this unit during their debates.

CRITICAL THINKING SKILLS Categorising

Ask students to read the first two paragraphs carefully. Highlight the fact that they will need to categorize information whenever they conduct research as part of their studies. Ask them to look at the questions in the yellow box and to attempt to answer them. They can then check their answers in pairs before reading on to find out whether they were right.

ANSWERS
Comparisons activity
Q1 They are all animals.
Q2 They are domestic pets.
Q3 They are young animals.

Now ask them to read the *Salient characteristics* section and to try the *Categorising* activity. Alert them to the fact that they probably won't be able to identify a commonality in all of them, as they may not have encountered some of the words, but encourage them to have a guess when they aren't sure. Again, they should check their answers in pairs before feeding back to the class.

ANSWERS
Categorising activity
a bodies of water
b nationalities
c animal habitats
d science subjects
e seven-letter words
f verbs with the prefix *de-*
g words containing *eve*
h cognitive (thinking) skills
I inflammatory conditions of bodily organs
j palindromes: words that read the same backwards and forwards
k terms that refer to the development of a soil profile
l multiples of seven
m forms of government
n collective nouns for types of animal

You might like to refer students to their dictionaries at this point, so that they can look up any words they were unsure about. They can then read the final paragraph. Be prepared to field any questions they may have.

UNIT 1 GATHERING

Student name: _____

Date: _____

Unit assignment: Planning a study group

25 points: Excellent achievement. Student successfully fulfills the expectation for this part of the assignment with little or no room for improvement.

20 points: Good achievement. Student fulfills the expectation for this part of the assignment, but with occasional errors and hesitancy.

15 points: Satisfactory achievement. Student needs some work to fulfill the expectation for this part of the assignment, but shows some effort.

5 points: Poor achievement. Student does not fulfill the expectation for this part of the assignment.

	25 points	20 points	15 points	10 points	0 points
The student interrupts appropriately.					
The student uses modals in various functions.					
Phonology—The student uses appropriate intonation.					
The student uses binomials, where appropriate.					

Total: _____ /100

Comments:

Student name: _____

Date: _____

Unit assignment: Formulating a debate on banning violent electronic games

25 points: Excellent achievement. Student successfully fulfills the expectation for this part of the assignment with little or no room for improvement.

20 points: Good achievement. Student fulfills the expectation for this part of the assignment, but with occasional errors and hesitancy.

15 points: Satisfactory achievement. Student needs some work to fulfill the expectation for this part of the assignment, but shows some effort.

5 points: Poor achievement. Student does not fulfill the expectation for this part of the assignment.

	25 points	20 points	15 points	10 points	0 points
The student uses the language of agreeing and disagreeing.					
The student uses the appropriate degree of formality.					
Phonology—The student uses a linking /r/ sound where appropriate.					
The student includes some phrasal verbs from the course.					

Total: _____ /100

Comments:

Unit assignment checklist

Unit assignment checklist

UNIT 3 NOSTALGIA

Student name: _____

Date: _____

Unit assignment: Conducting a survey on memory

25 points: Excellent achievement. Student successfully fulfills the expectation for this part of the assignment with little or no room for improvement.

20 points: Good achievement. Student fulfills the expectation for this part of the assignment, but with occasional errors and hesitancy.

15 points: Satisfactory achievement. Student needs some work to fulfill the expectation for this part of the assignment, but shows some effort.

5 points: Poor achievement. Student does not fulfill the expectation for this part of the assignment.

	25 points	20 points	15 points	10 points	0 points
The student refers to and uses sources.					
The student uses approximation where appropriate.					
Phonology—The student uses juncture to connect words.					
The student includes some particulizer and exclusive adverbs.					

Total: _____ /100

Comments:

UNIT 4 RISK

Student name: _____

Date: _____

Unit assignment: Undertaking an informal risk assessment

25 points: Excellent achievement. Student successfully fulfills the expectation for this part of the assignment with little or no room for improvement.

20 points: Good achievement. Student fulfills the expectation for this part of the assignment, but with occasional errors and hesitancy.

15 points: Satisfactory achievement. Student needs some work to fulfill the expectation for this part of the assignment, but shows some effort.

5 points: Poor achievement. Student does not fulfill the expectation for this part of the assignment.

	25 points	20 points	15 points	10 points	0 points
The student uses conditionals to make predictions.					
The student manages the conversation effectively.					
Phonology—The student uses appropriate word stress.					
The student uses other structures to make predictions appropriately.					

Total: _____ /100

Comments:

Unit assignment checklist

Student name: _____

Date: _____

Unit assignment: Presenting a proposal of an action plan for an urban issue

25 points: Excellent achievement. Student successfully fulfills the expectation for this part of the assignment with little or no room for improvement.

20 points: Good achievement. Student fulfills the expectation for this part of the assignment, but with occasional errors and hesitancy.

15 points: Satisfactory achievement. Student needs some work to fulfill the expectation for this part of the assignment, but shows some effort.

5 points: Poor achievement. Student does not fulfill the expectation for this part of the assignment.

	25 points	20 points	15 points	10 points	0 points
The student supports their proposal effectively.					
The student uses academic verbs where appropriate.					
Phonology—The student uses appropriate contrastive stress.					
The student uses the appropriate connotation of target words.					

Total: _____ /100

Comments:

UNIT 6 LEGACY

Student name: _____

Date: _____

Unit assignment: Making a speech about a person who has left a legacy

25 points: Excellent achievement. Student successfully fulfills the expectation for this part of the assignment with little or no room for improvement.

20 points: Good achievement. Student fulfills the expectation for this part of the assignment, but with occasional errors and hesitancy.

15 points: Satisfactory achievement. Student needs some work to fulfill the expectation for this part of the assignment, but shows some effort.

5 points: Poor achievement. Student does not fulfill the expectation for this part of the assignment.

	25 points	20 points	15 points	10 points	0 points
The student repeats grammatical forms for emphasis.					
The student uses contrastive pairs for emphasis.					
Phonology—The student pauses for dramatic emphasis.					
The student uses inversion for emphasis.					

Total: _____ /100

Comments:

UNIT 7 EXPANSE

Student name: _____

Date: _____

Unit assignment: Organizing a cultural program

25 points: Excellent achievement. Student successfully fulfills the expectation for this part of the assignment with little or no room for improvement.

20 points: Good achievement. Student fulfills the expectation for this part of the assignment, but with occasional errors and hesitancy.

15 points: Satisfactory achievement. Student needs some work to fulfill the expectation for this part of the assignment, but shows some effort.

5 points: Poor achievement. Student does not fulfill the expectation for this part of the assignment.

	25 points	20 points	15 points	10 points	0 points
The student uses appropriate attitude adverbials.					
The student makes suggestions using modal verbs.					
Phonology—The student uses appropriate word stress.					
The student uses checking phrases appropriately.					

Total: _____ /100

Comments:

UNIT 8 | CHANGE

Student name: _____

Date: _____

Unit assignment: Holding a debate about educational changes

25 points: Excellent achievement. Student successfully fulfills the expectation for this part of the assignment with little or no room for improvement.

20 points: Good achievement. Student fulfills the expectation for this part of the assignment, but with occasional errors and hesitancy.

15 points: Satisfactory achievement. Student needs some work to fulfill the expectation for this part of the assignment, but shows some effort.

5 points: Poor achievement. Student does not fulfill the expectation for this part of the assignment.

	25 points	20 points	15 points	10 points	0 points
The student adds points effectively to an argument.					
The student uses gradeable adjectives appropriately.					
Phonology—The student uses appropriate intonation and sentence stress.					
The student expresses change appropriately.					

Total: _____ /100

Comments:

UNIT 9 FLOW

Student name: _____

Date: _____

Unit assignment: Making an advertisement supported by visuals

25 points: Excellent achievement. Student successfully fulfills the expectation for this part of the assignment with little or no room for improvement.

20 points: Good achievement. Student fulfills the expectation for this part of the assignment, but with occasional errors and hesitancy.

15 points: Satisfactory achievement. Student needs some work to fulfill the expectation for this part of the assignment, but shows some effort.

5 points: Poor achievement. Student does not fulfill the expectation for this part of the assignment.

	25 points	20 points	15 points	10 points	0 points
The student softens their criticism of other people's ideas using personal position.					
The student softens their criticism using modal verbs.					
Phonology—The student uses intonation to express hesitation and doubt.					
The student uses irregular plurals accurately.					

Total: _____ /100

Comments:

UNIT 10 CONFLICT

Student name: _____

Date: _____

Unit assignment: Role-playing mini-conflict situations

25 points: Excellent achievement. Student successfully fulfills the expectation for this part of the assignment with little or no room for improvement.

20 points: Good achievement. Student fulfills the expectation for this part of the assignment, but with occasional errors and hesitancy.

15 points: Satisfactory achievement. Student needs some work to fulfill the expectation for this part of the assignment, but shows some effort.

5 points: Poor achievement. Student does not fulfill the expectation for this part of the assignment.

	25 points	20 points	15 points	10 points	0 points
The student reformulates and monitors to manage conflict.					
The student uses hedging and boosting.					
Phonology—The student links words fluently.					
The student uses the correct linkers.					

Total: _____ /100

Comments:

UNIT 1 Gathering

Vocabulary preview

1 professor 2 coordinator 3 handouts
4 nominated 5 participation 6 objectives
7 figure out 8 chaotic

LISTENING 1 Three meetings

Listening

1

Meeting 1—a lecture
The purpose is for a professor to give students an overview of the Sociology 101 course.
We can assume that this is the first meeting between the professor and the students, and that the students are not fully aware of the lecture protocols. The interaction level is fairly formal, with the professor leading the meeting.
Meeting 2—a seminar (or a semi-formal, academic get-together)
This meeting occurs in an academic setting in a classroom or similar interior space. There is a lead speaker who monitors the pattern of discussion. The purpose is to set up a group project, delegating roles to the participants.
Meeting 3—a seminar (or a semi-formal, academic get-together)
This meeting appears to be the initial meeting for students new to a university debating society. The speaker introduces the purpose of the debating society and formally covers a list of points.

2

1 sociology
2 one don't—phones making noises
3 One woman queries the project due date. One woman doesn't have a handout. One woman is in the wrong group and leaves.
4 She suggests dividing the work into three sections and that two people take a section each.
5 It's a great way to integrate into campus life, make new friends, and meet other people with similar interests. In addition, taking an active role in the debating society can help your speaking and presentation skills, help you think critically and analytically, and build your resumé.
6 an open door policy

Critical thinking skill

1

1 c   2 b   3 b

LISTENING 2 Getting from *you and me*, to *we*

Listening

1

1 a seminar (or academic discussion group)
2 The speakers consist of a professor, who is leading the topic, and students, who are making contributions to the topic.
3 Group dynamics is about the way speakers interact in a group.

2

b

Critical thinking skill

1

1 forming 2 storming 3 performing
4 storming 5 norming 6 norming
7 performing 8 adjourning

2

1 performing 2 norming 3 forming
4 performing

Language development: Binomials

1

all or nothing; cut and dried; give or take; loud and clear; pure and simple; show and tell; time and effort; ups and downs

2

1 time and effort   5 ups and downs
2 show and tell   6 cut and dried
3 loud and clear   7 pure and simple
4 all or nothing   8 give or take

SPEAKING Planning a study group

Pronunciation skill

1

1 A: worry   B: suspicion
2 A: surprise   B: indifference
3 A: anger   B: sarcasm

Speaking skill

1 Sorry to interrupt, but …
2 May I say something here?
3 Do you mind if I say something here?

SPEAKING TASK

Plan

1

1 three 2 a study hall (next to the cafeteria) 3 90 minutes, once a week

UNIT 2 Games

Vocabulary preview

1 stimulating 2 motivate 3 likelihood
4 reward 5 Neurologists 6 dopamine
7 addiction 8 ultimatum

LISTENING 1 Video games: Lessons for life

Listening

1

1 not given 2 true 3 false 4 false 5 true
6 true

2

1 achieving long- and short-term aims
2 reward for effort
3 learning from feedback
4 enhanced visual attention
5 creativity

Critical thinking skill

1

Points 2, 3, 4, 6, and 7 contain key information.

2

1 K, E, E   2 K, E, E   3 E, E, K

Developing critical thinking

The sentence summarizes point 2.

LISTENING 2 Game theory

Before you listen

1 mathematical 2 losses 3 decisions
4 cooperate 5 economics
6 negotiations 7 diplomacy 8 engage

Listening

The ultimatum – money-sharing situation
The assurance situation – The Stag Hunt
The anti-coordination situation – the game of chicken
The Prisoner's Dilemma – why people cooperate

Critical thinking skill

1

1 A   3 U   5 A   7 A   9 A
2 U   4 A   6 U   8 U   10 U

2

The point/topic/title
The anti-coordination situation
The game of chicken / Hawk–dove game
The most important and relevant information, plus examples
The principle of the game is that each player prefers not to yield to the other, but if they don't yield, they get the worst possible outcome.
A situation in which there is competition for a shared resource and the contestants can choose either resolution or conflict.
Real-world application is in the world of negotiation in international diplomacy, where neither side wants to back down or lose face, but risks total loss if they don't.
The source of the information
Ross Cressman, book, *The Stability Concept of Evolutionary Game Theory*, 1992.
The point/topic/title
The Prisoner's Dilemma. A mathematical explanation of why people cooperate.
The most important and relevant information, plus examples
Each prisoner has a choice. He can remain silent, or confess and tell the police his partner is guilty—each prisoner knows that the other has the same choice.
The real dilemma—the best strategy for each prisoner individually is to confess and blame the crime on the other. But it could provide a worse outcome.
Real-world application is about cooperating even when something isn't in your best interests.
The source of the information
Albert W. Tucker, book, *Contributions to the Theory of Games*, 1950

Language development: Prepositional verbs

1

1 with   3 for   5 on   7 to
2 to   4 in   6 for   8 for

2

1 glancing <u>quickly</u> through
2 refers <u>mainly</u> to
3 look <u>only</u> at
4 listen <u>carefully</u> to (Note that it's grammatically possible for *carefully* to come at the end of this sentence, too.)

Language development: Phrasal verbs

1

1 prepositional verb
2 phrasal verb
3 phrasal verb
4 prepositional verb
5 phrasal verb
6 phrasal verb

2

1 constitutes
2 evaluates
3 quit
4 examines
5 fabricate
6 discuss

3

1 *stipulates*—academic text (utilizes a formal single word rather than a phrasal verb)
2 *ascertain*—academic text (utilizes a formal single word rather than a phrasal verb)
3 BOTH—The sentence could be from a semi-formal magazine video game review. *Organizing* is more neutral.
4 *support, increases*—academic text (utilizes a formal single word rather than a phrasal verb)
5 BOTH—The sentence could be spoken in an informal/semi-formal context.
6 *manage*—academic text (utilizes a formal single word rather than a phrasal verb)
7 *step up, take part*—Reference to "she" suggests this is a spoken, informal context.

SPEAKING Formulating a debate on banning violent electronic games

Pronunciation skill

1

1 I'm principally a lecture<u>r at</u> the university's Entertainment Technology Center.
2 He pinpoints video games as an area that gives us greate<u>r i</u>nsight into how learning takes place.
3 No one can learn unless they a<u>re a</u>ble to connect consequences to actions, especially when the consequences a<u>re i</u>n the distant future.
4 In real life the<u>re are</u>, I read anyway, that the<u>re are</u> few real zero-sum games.
5 The<u>re are</u> two outcomes to the stag hunt. Either both hunters hunt the stag together, or both hunters hunt rabbits on thei<u>r own</u>.
6 Two drivers drive towards each othe<u>r on</u> a collision course.

Speaking skill

1

Statement	Student 1	Student 2
We can become better drivers by playing video games.	✓	✓
Gaming can improve your creativity.	✓	✗
It's better to cooperate in the Prisoner's Dilemma situation.	✓	✗
The best outcome is only possible if you don't cooperate.	✗	✓

2

The first dialogue is an informal conversation. A key marker for the informality is the line, "Yeah, definitely." The second dialogue has no markers of informality so it is more likely to be a formal debate.

UNIT 3 Nostalgia

Vocabulary preview

1

1 remember
2 have forgotten it
3 having bad memories of
4 forget about it
5 brought back
6 help (or make) you remember
7 help (or make) you remember
8 remember (good times)

2

Remember: recall, get flashbacks, evoke, trigger, jog your memory, reminisce
Forget: slip your mind, put something behind you

3

get flashbacks, put something behind you

LISTENING 1 How to deal with homesickness

Listening

1

Nicola: d and f **Amanda**: c and e **Chloe**: a and b

2

Student	Feel when first arrived?	Feel afterwards?
Nicola	Felt like an outsider, anxious and insecure. Was forgetful in terms of course work.	Settled and calm.
Amanda	Had difficulty eating and sleeping. Felt ill—dizzy and had headaches.	Ready to embrace her new environment.
Chloe	Felt depressed and disinterested. Lacked confidence.	Felt more at ease.

Critical thinking skill

1

different lifestyle, people, & weather and *language barriers* are causes of homesickness rather than effects.

2

1 Suffered physical symptoms: loss of appetite, headaches & dizziness
2 Suffered psychological symptoms: felt anxious & insecure, sleeping problems, difficulty concentrating, forgetfulness, depression
3 Studies were affected: missed lectures, scored low grades, lost interest in course, neglected research assignments, failed exams
4 Social life was affected: stopped going to clubs, lost confidence

3

Nicola: 2, 3 **Amanda**: 1 **Chloe**: 2, 3, 4

LISTENING 2 Memory and smell:

Critical thinking skill: Representative samples

1

Willander

1 no **2** Average age was 75 **3** Participants' childhood was a long time ago—better test of how powerful the memory prompts are.

Toffolo *et al*

1 no **2** All female, all healthy **3** More women than men suffer from PTSD

Language development: Approximation

1

1 round <u>about</u> 2 a little <u>over</u> 3 up <u>to</u>
4 something <u>like</u> 5 or <u>so</u> 6 just short <u>of</u>

2

Approximately: round about; something like; or so
Less than, but including: up to; just short of
More: a little over

3

1 **Up to** 50 students per course.
2 **under / nearly / almost / around / round about** 10 seconds
3 **(just) over / upwards of / somewhere in the region of / something like** 100 scientific papers
4 I completed the test in **less than / under** 30 minutes.
5 Zara scored **nearly / almost** 90% on the test. She's very smart!
6 The university is relatively new; it was built **less than / under** 20 years ago.

Language development: Particulizer and exclusive adverbs

1

1 particularly
2 solely
3 precisely
4 especially
5 Mostly
6 Only

SPEAKING Conducting a survey on memory

Pronunciation skill

1 The student longs fo<u>r a</u>nd becomes distresse<u>d o</u>ver the <u>loss of</u> wha<u>t i</u>s familia<u>r a</u>nd secure.
2 According to the Office of National Statistics, o<u>ne in</u> five students dro<u>p out</u> after the first yea<u>r of</u> study.
3 When <u>I</u> came last year <u>it</u> was the first ti<u>me I'd</u> ever been to the U.K.
4 What <u>I</u> would <u>advise is</u> to <u>get out</u> there <u>a</u>nd make contact with the peopl<u>e a</u>round you.
5 In fact, I looke<u>d at</u> photos from wh<u>en I</u> wa<u>s in Au</u>stralia.
6 I<u>n an e</u>xperiment ai<u>ming to</u> investigat<u>e a</u>versive memories, similar t<u>o those e</u>xperienced by PTSD patients …

STUDY SKILLS Listening to extended lectures

Scenario

Possible answer

Imran needs more listening practice. As he finds accents problematic, he could listen to local media and watch the TV news for that region each day. He could also join some social clubs with other local students. Imran should focus on taking notes of only the key words and key points. He could form or join a study group to help consolidate his ideas about things he thought he had heard, or wasn't sure about. He could also practice taking notes from online presentations which feature a multi-media mix.

UNIT 4 Risk

Vocabulary preview

1

1 fatalities 2 run 3 take 4 poses 5 steel
6 unregulated 7 faced 8 say 9 odds
10 on-the-job

3

1 Smokers have a high risk of getting cancer.
2 If you eat too much, you run the risk of having health problems.
3 If you don't lock up your bicycle, you risk losing it.

Rule: *Risk* (verb) is followed by the *-ing* form of the verb, not the infinitive. *Risk* (noun) is followed by the preposition *of* and the *-ing* form of the verb.

LISTENING 1 The world's most dangerous jobs

Listening

2

construction worker, logger, fisherman, window cleaner

Critical thinking skill

1 window cleaner 2 fisherman
3 logger 4 logger 5 fisherman 6 logger
7 fisherman / window cleaner 8 logger

LISTENING 2 What is acceptable risk?

Listening

1

The student in the audio says that acceptable risk describes an unwanted event that can meet any one of three categories.
The professor's purpose is to **explain** the concept of acceptable risk.

2

1 F 2 T 3 T 4 T 5 F 6 T 7 NG 8 T

Critical thinking skill

2

2

3

Checked sentences should be: 1, 3, 5, 7

Language development: Nominalization

1

active (adj)   explode (verb)
dangerous (adj)   measure (verb)
disappoint (verb)   organize (verb)
drown (verb)   safe (adj)

2

achievement   generosity
decision   insecurity
expansion   involvement
expectation   uncertainty

SPEAKING Undertaking an informal risk assessment

Pronunciation skill

1 destruction; the second to last
2 dangerous; unstressed
3 impossible; unstressed
4 sunglasses; first
5 well-behaved; unstressed

Speaking skill

CT: 2, 4, 6, 9 ST: 1, 3, 8, 10 CB: 5, 7

UNIT 5 Sprawl

Vocabulary preview

1

City infrastructure: drainage system, freeway
Urban issues: urban sprawl, urban decay
People in the city: pedestrian, merchant
Places in or around the city: urban block, suburb
City transportation: trolley, streetcar

2

1 freeway 2 drainage system 3 urban decay
4 urban sprawl 5 trolley, streetcar
6 pedestrian 7 merchant 8 urban
block 9 suburb

LISTENING 1 Cars and cities

Critical thinking skill

1

1 a   2 b   3 b

LISTENING 2 Making cities more liveable

Listening

1 c   2 a   3 b

Critical thinking skill

1 & 2

Criteria	Copenhagen	New Delhi
Resilience	Current planning includes green spaces such as parks, gardens, and trees. Lighting has been invested in as a well-lit environment fosters creativity and social activity.	A plan to bring the citizens back into the city centre. Reduce the amount of traffic in the centre to build new parks.
Inclusiveness	Part of the urban development process includes consultation with residents. Projects create a sense of community for residents.	Develop new public areas. Rejuvenating canals and building walkways and cycle paths. They want to include people from all walks of life. It will not be too expensive for anyone.
Authenticity	Good quality architecture gives people a sense of pride in the city.	Encouraging civic pride by promoting heritage. The building of the Guru Tegh Bahadur memorial. The teachings of the gurus are engraved on huge monoliths in the park.

Language development: Connotation

1

1 cramped –, populous ≈, overcrowded – (different connotation: populous)
2 reckon ≈, contemplate ≈, reflect ≈ (different connotation: reckon)
3 growth ≈, expansion ≈, sprawl – (different connotation: sprawl)
4 struggle –, strive +, endeavor + (different connotation: struggle)
5 ample +, enough ≈, abundant + (different connotation: enough)
6 push out –, expand ≈, extend ≈ (different connotation: push out)

2

1 c   2 b   3 a   4 a   5 c

Language development: Academic verbs

1

1 c   2 f   3 a   4 d   5 b   6 e

2

shift: consciously change your way of thinking;
vary: make changes in something in order to give more diversity;
transform: make something or someone completely different;

develop: change land for a particular purpose;
evolve: progressively change over a period of time;
adapt: change your ideas or behavior so that you can deal with a new situation

3
1 vary 2 adapt 3 evolved 4 transformed

SPEAKING Presenting a proposal of an action plan for an urban issue

Pronunciation skill

2
1 Our current city planning isn't only about architecture; it also includes green spaces.
2 New Delhi isn't India's largest city; it's the largest metropolitan area.
3 If parks are the lungs, then water is the blood of a city!

Speaking skill

1
1 **Proposal**: Make the subway more accessible. **Problem**: Few people travel by subway due to limited accessibility.
2 **Proposal**: Go to the event by bus. **Problem**: If they don't, they may arrive late.
3 **Proposal**: Increase the price of public transportation. **Problem**: The service is suffering from financial problems.
4 **Proposal**: Introduce one ticket for all modes of public transportation. **Problem**: Not enough people are traveling by public transportation.

STUDY SKILLS Recording achievement

Scenario

Possible answer
I might include a monthly schedule of my activities. I would keep track of events that I have participated in, whether they are academic or non-academic, and reflect on how they may have contributed to my overall personal development. I might also include an emotions diary, and see how my mood affected my productivity. I also might include essay drafts and compare how my thought processes change across an assignment.

UNIT 6 Legacy

Vocabulary preview

1
1 launch, unveiling
2 to revolutionize, to change the face of
3 to address, to deal with
4 to hand down, to pass on
5 achievement, success
6 to convey, to express
7 to stand to, to be likely to
8 ritual, custom

3
1 launch
2 revolutionized / changed the face of
3 address / deal with
4 handed down / passed on

5 success / achievement
6 convey / express
7 stand to / are likely to
8 customs

LISTENING 1 Family food legacies

Critical thinking skill

1
Information: A meal is more than just about food—it's about civilizing people.; A family routine involves discussion about a task.; There are similar patterns of sharing ideas at the dinner table across countries.; Rich and delicious memories connected to eating at home.; A ritual makes a family feel united.
Source name: Robin Fox; Barbara Feise et al.; Russell Belk; The class in the audio track lecture; n/a.
Publication name: n/a; n/a; "Sharing," Journal of Consumer Research, UoC Press; Online forum; Some reports
Primary (P) / Secondary (S) source?: S; S; S; P; S
Authoritative source?: ✓ Anthropologisr at Rutgers University. U.S.; ✓ University of Illinois, U.S.; n/a; no; n/a
Valid research participant base?: n/a; ✓ 182,000 youngsters; n/a; n/a; n/a

LISTENING 2 Technology legacies

Before you listen

3
a Tim Berners-Lee (inventor of the World Wide Web; British, b. 1955)
b Steve Jobs (co-founder of Apple Inc.; American, 1955–2011)
c Alan Turing (early computer scientist who developed computer programs; British, 1912–1954)

Listening

Student 1: Steve Jobs; Apple changed the face of modern computing.
Student 2: Alan Turing; He developed the first computer.
Student 3: Tim Berners-Lee; He invented the World Wide Web.

Critical thinking skill

1

Inventor	A citation that uses a passive construction
Apple®/Steve Jobs	It's been argued that Apple and Steve Jobs were responsible for bringing computer icons and the mouse to a greater public.
Alan Turing	Turing is considered the father of modern computing.
Tim Berners-Lee	Berners-Lee is credited also with building the first web browser, creating the first web server, and …

Language development: Inversion

1
1 only 2 no 3 Never 4 now 5 sooner

2
1 Never again will there be a technological revolution.

2 Not only did Apple® revolutionize the phone industry, but they also created the tablet industry.
3 No sooner do phone companies release the latest model than they bring a newer one out.
4 Not until Microsoft® Windows was launched were computers available to the general public.
5 Rarely do you meet anyone nowadays who doesn't have a computer.
6 Only by reading their biography and using their product can you understand someone's technological legacy.
7 Only recently has my family started to pass on family mealtime rituals.

Language development: Collocations: *way*

1
1 on   3 into   5 in   7 have
2 long   4 go   6 give   8 toward

2
a have a way with b give way to c on its way d went a long way toward e a long way f in a bad way g way into h the way to go

3
1, 4, 5, 6, and 7 are the most informal. 2, 3, and 8 could be used in more formal settings.

SPEAKING Making a speech about a person who has left a legacy

Pronunciation skill

2
1 A family mealtime ritual could be a symbolic act: // it could involve objects, // or it could be conversations.
2 Sure, it was the size of a room, // and today's tablets can fit in your pocket // but still, it's pretty impressive.
3 No sooner do phone companies release the latest model // than a newer one comes out.
4 Only by reading someone's biography // and using their product // can you understand their technological legacy.

Speaking skill

1
1 repetition of grammar   2 contrastive pairs
3 repetition of grammar   4 repetition of grammar   5 repetition of grammar
6 contrastive pairs

UNIT 7 Expanse

Vocabulary preview

1
1 transcontinental 2 colossal/gargantuan/vast 3 remoteness 4 extensive
5 considerable/extensive 6 aloof
7 proximity 8 gargantuan/vast 9 vast
10 high up

2
The words *colossal*, *gargantuan*, and *vast* are synonyms for *enormous*.

LISTENING 1 The Trans-Siberian Railway

Listening

1 9289—the distance of the journey between Moscow and Vladivostok is 9289 km.
2 seven—the length of the journey between Moscow and Vladivostok is seven days
3 two—the journey passes through two continents
4 ten—it took ten months to travel from European Russia to Siberia by horse and cart
5 seventy-two—the same journey later took 72 hours by train and it was the estimated excursion time to China, Turkey, or Poland to buy goods
6 eighty—the train transports 80% of all goods
7 1.5 million—1.5 million people are employed by Russian Railways
8 twelve—the average waiting time in Novosibirsk for a connection home is 12 hours

Critical thinking skill

1

	Statement 1: Russia is a huge country.	Statement 2: Russian people are friendly and interesting.
Do you have any experience or knowledge of the topic?	Answers will vary. Answer will be yes for most students.	Answers will vary.
Does the statement fit with your experience or knowledge?	Possible answer: Yes, I know Russia is the biggest country in the world.	Answers will vary.
Is there any language to signal opinion?	No	to my mind
What evidence is presented (if any)?	The railway line that crosses it is 9,289 km. (and passes through seven time zones and two continents).	Russian people on the train treated the speaker like family and offered him food.
Does the evidence prove the statement? Why or why not?	Yes. 9,289 km. is measurable and can be compared against measurements of other countries.	Possible answer: No. This is just one person's experience of a very small proportion of the Russian population.
Is it fact or opinion?	Fact	Opinion

2
1 F   2 O   3 F   4 F   5 F   6 O

LISTENING 2 Why do people climb mountains?

Listening

All adjectives correspond except *exhausting*.

Critical thinking skil

1
Statements 1, 2, 4, and 6 require justification.

2
1 Justification—One of the factors of enjoyment is cooperation.
2 Justification—(Both life and climbing) have barriers that have to be overcome.
4 Justification—It compels us to explore and extend our physical limitations.
6 Justification—We feel like artists and have the same feeling of originality when we create a new route.

Language development: Attitude adverbials

1 **Not surprisingly**, most of the quality road systems are based around Moscow and Saint Petersburg.
2 **Understandably**, the remoteness of this vast land area isolated many groups of Russians across two continents, making it very difficult to rule as a nation.
3 I **personally** believe the Russians are friendly people.
4 Climbing is **undoubtedly** a dangerous pursuit.
5 **Ideally**, you should go climbing with a team.
6 **Honestly**, I have never seen anything as beautiful as a sunrise from the top of a mountain crest.

Language development: Abstract nouns

1
1 possibility; existence; development
2 kindness
3 importance
4 inactivity; unemployment; hardship
5 unity
6 satisfaction
7 achievement

2

-ment: develop, employ,	-ence: exist
-action: satisfy	-ance: important
-y: unite	-ship: hard achieve
-ness: kind	-ity: possible, active

3
1 inactivity 2 unemployment 3 satisfaction 4 existence 5 achievement 6 development

Pronunciation skill

1

1 **poss**ible	possi**bil**ity
2 **sat**isfy	satis**fac**tion
3 e**xist**	e**xis**tence
4 a**chieve**	a**chieve**ment
5 de**vel**op	de**vel**opment
6 im**por**tant	im**por**tance
7 in**ac**tive	inac**tiv**ity
8 em**ploy**	em**ploy**ment

2
-ity and -tion endings cause a change in stress. With nouns ending in -ity, the stress moves to the syllable before -ity.
With nouns ending in -ion, the stress moves to the second to last syllable.

Speaking skill

1
Expressions used in the discussion:
I'd like to suggest that; Are you happy with that?; I think perhaps; What do you think about that?; I think we should; What would be wrong with doing that?; Perhaps we could; They decide to include a brief clarification of the theory.

STUDY SKILLS Organizing your personal study online

Scenario

Possible answer

Haru could develop better self-study strategies to organize his time more effectively. He needs to schedule his week so that he has time available for research. He needs to learn how to use academic search engines. He needs more self-discipline not to get distracted by other Internet media while online. He also needs to find a suitable space for studying. This might mean negotiating with the other people in his house to give him quiet time or finding an empty classroom to use.

UNIT 8 Change

Vocabulary preview

1
1 frequently   2 comes out of an egg
3 under the ground   4 has offspring
5 outside its body   6 it is expected to live   7 buying or selling something
8 problem with no apparent solution

2
fluctuates

LISTENING 1 Metamorphosis—the secrets behind nature's amazing change

Listening

1

1 13 or 17	3 3	5 1.5	7 68
2 5	4 100	6 20	

Critical thinking skill

1

Student annotation may vary. The actual audio script is:

After **biding their time** underground for 17 years, these **creatures rise from** the ground and **march like zombies** to the nearest tree. **Starting to climb, they begin their final journey to unleash millions** of their kind into **just** a few acres of land. … **It's the remarkable life cycle of the periodical cicada** that we will look at today in order to consider **a conundrum** that has puzzled experts **for decades.** Why do they wait so long to complete their metamorphosis? And why do they all **appear** at the same time? Let's start by looking at the 17-year variety's **peculiar** life cycle.

2

For the maximized language, see the words in bold in the answer key for exercise 1. The speaker wants to convey the sense of scale of this phenomenon.

LISTENING 2 A global tax on changing money?

Before you listen

2

1 lending 2 speculation 3 risky 4 profit

Listening

1 b   2 b   3 a   4 b   5 b

Critical thinking skill

1

1 goes up; massive impact; people's pockets
2 put more; slow down; hurt
3 huge amounts; relying on; create and develop

2

1 negative   2 discourages   3 a bad thing

Language development: Gradeable adjectives

1

1 very 2 a little 3 practically 4 a little 5 a little

2

1 Not only is technology a forum for sharing and presenting existing knowledge, it also provides a ~~very~~ unique opportunity to create new knowledge. This creates superior knowledge.
2 There is an absolutely infinite choice of learning tools using technology, it's true. But it's also true that a ~~quite~~ huge choice of possible distractions exist. Social media, instant messaging, and online games can detract from learning.
3 Face-to-face learning is ~~virtually~~ important for many reasons, such as group work and real-world application of tasks. It's almost impossible to reproduce these conditions online.
4 Businesses and commercial interests are mainly responsible for many technological changes in the classroom. Teachers and students play a ~~very~~ miniscule part in these changes.

SPEAKING Holding a debate about educational changes

Pronunciation skill

1 B: I had <u>no</u> idea what the professor was talking about.
2 B: I didn't take <u>any</u> notes on the first lecture.
3 B: I don't think <u>anybody</u> knows if this tax will work.
4 B: Yes, but who would <u>enforce</u> those laws to decide where the money goes?

Speaking skill

a Moreover; 5 **b** I would like to argue; 1
c more than sufficient; 3 **d** My main reason; 2 **e** What is more; 4

UNIT 9 Flow

Vocabulary preview

1 aquatic   6 contamination
2 Evaporation   7 compelling
3 contemplating   8 Intrinsic motivation
4 displacement   9 subjective
5 sobering   10 economic stimulus

LISTENING 1 Not worth a dam

Before you listen

2

1 irrigation
2 hydroelectric power
3 renewable energy
4 significant controversy
5 environmental costs
6 river ecosystems

Listening

1 She is speaking to committee members.
2 She is asking participants to reconsider a dam project.
3 She gives four reasons: building costs; displacement of the local population; environmental damage; and ineffective water storage.
4 (I urge you to reconsider this project for the good of our people, for the good of our community, and for the good of our land.) Thank you for your attention.

Critical thinking skill

1

Sentences 1, 3, 4, 5, and 7 should be checked.

2

a 5   b 1   c 3   d 7   e 4

LISTENING 2 The concept of flow

Language development: Irregular plurals

1

1 hypotheses 2 series 3 species
4 halves 5 bases 6 kilos 7 heroes
8 audiences 9 proximities
10 metamorphoses 11 stimuli
12 conundrums 13 aircraft 14 bogs
15 youths 16 reservoirs 17 statistics 18 knowledge

2

1 no singular form   5 no singular form
2 criterion   6 no singular form
3 no singular form   7 phenomenon
4 knife   8 no singular form

3

1 suggest 2 have closed 3 both are possible 4 are 5 are 6 produces 7 it 8 both are possible 9 are 10 both are possible

Language development: Words in context—working with concordance data

1 verb or noun
2 *continuous, free*
3 *correspondence, noise, information, funds, fuel, tunes, air, blood, cash, commerce*
4 *the/a + flow + of + noun*
5 *a flow of cash* and *the flow of commerce*

SPEAKING Making an advertisement supported by visuals

Pronunciation skill

1

agree: yes; I guess so; well, OK
disagree: no; I don't think so; I'm not sure

2

1 a   2 b   3 b   4 a   5 a   6 a

Speaking skill

1

Possible answers
1 You may have done the wrong exercise.
2 It seems to me that your conclusion is confusing.
3 I find it difficult to understand your accent.
4 It seems we aren't communicating well.
5 I wonder if it might be better for you to do it again.
6 You might not have quoted the source correctly.

STUDY SKILLS Exam techniques

Scenario

Possible answer

I think avoiding other students who make you feel nervous and anxious about exams is beneficial.

UNIT 10 Conflict

Vocabulary preview

1

1 alluding to; criticize 2 aftermath
3 rivalry; animosity 4 violent
5 loyalty 6 struggle 7 accusation

2

Negative: criticize, aftermath, animosity, violent, struggle, accusation
Positive or neutral: alluding to, rivalry, loyalty

LISTENING 1 Conflict of interest

Before you listen

1

b (Although a covers part of the topic, b is the more comprehensive summary.)

Critical thinking skill

1

1 utilitarian	3 egotistical
2 golden rule	4 *prima facie*

2

a 2 b 3 c 4 d 1

LISTENING 2 "The Sporting Spirit"

Before you listen

1 negative 2 attack: lash out at, criticize: lambast 3 It sounds as though it will give a one-sided view.

Listening

a 2 b 3 c 4 d 1 e 6 f 5

Critical thinking skill

1

1 ✓ 2 ✓ 3 ✗ 4 ✓ 5 ✓ 6 ✓

2

Exact wording of answer may vary. The answer comes from this section of the audio script:

… Yet, we feel that he contradicts himself in the closing part when he writes *"I do not, of course, suggest that sport is one of the main causes of international rivalry."* He starts by saying it's an unfailing cause and concludes by stating that it's not one of the main causes. We feel that nationalism and tribalism can come out during sports events. But, the cause isn't the sport itself—the rivalries are already there.

Language development: Hedging and boosting

1

More assertive: certainly, without a doubt, for certain, inevitably, categorically, unquestionably
Less assertive: apparently, in some respects, partially, as a general rule, seemingly, in a sense, likely

2

1 Now, this is a small dilemma, and it's **unquestionably** easy for most people to solve it.
2 An action that produces a good result **may** be morally right.
3 Faced with difficult choices and internal conflict, these frameworks, I believe, help us **in some respects**.
4 We **should** remind ourselves that without electricity, nothing would work.
5 The threat is out there, and it's **seemingly** real.

Language development: Using the correct linker

1

1 Firstly 2 at first 3 at last 4 On the contrary 5 on the other hand

SPEAKING Role-playing mini-conflict situations

Pronunciation skill

1

1 I'd like to offer framework<u>s and</u> theories.
2 I see your poin<u>t ab</u>out this.
3 That exam was awful—if I pa<u>ss it</u>, I'll be amazed.
4 Nothing <u>at all</u>.
5 The team walke<u>d out</u> of the stadium.
6 I'd like to say tha<u>t I</u> agree.

Speaking skill

2

Some examples of reformulation and monitoring from the discourse:
So you're saying …; Well, technically …; As a matter of fact, …; In other words, …

CRITICAL THINKING SKILLS
Categorising

Comparisons activity
Q1 They are all animals.
Q2 They are domestic pets.
Q3 They are young animals.
Categorising activity
a bodies of water
b nationalities
c animal habitats
d science subjects
e seven-letter words
f verbs with the prefix *de-*
g words containing *eve*
h cognitive (thinking) skills
i inflammatory conditions of bodily organs
j palindromes: words that read the same backwards and forwards
k terms that refer to the development of a soil profile
l multiples of seven
m forms of government
n collective nouns for types of animal